Creative Eating

Simple & Healthy Recipes for a Busy Lifestyle!

LILLIAN EASTERLY-SMITH

WITH DEANNA CATALANO & KELLY HAWKINS

Copyright © 2019 by Lillian Easterly-Smith

LifeCare Publishing is a branch of
LifeCare Christian Center
A non-profit faith-based ministry
www.LifeCareChristianCenter.org
info.lifecarecc@gmail.com
Westland, MI USA

Mission Statement

LifeCare's mission is to provide opportunities as a care center that offer help, hope and healing in relationships and individually in body, soul and spirit through various resources including counseling, coaching, spiritual direction, classes, transformation groups, seminars, healing weekends and other professional interventions in multiple locations as well as training others to do so worldwide.

Cover design by Kelly Hawkins

All rights reserved. No part of this publication may be reproduced, stored in a retrieval system, or transmitted in any form or by any means – electronic, mechanical, photocopy, recording, or any other – except for brief quotations in printed or digital reviews without the prior written permission of the publisher.

ISBN: 9781072116271

CONTENTS

Welcome	5
Tips from the Author	7
Smoothies	15
Salads	27
Main Dishes	43
Soups	65
Side Dishes	77
Desserts	87
Snacks	111
Essential Oils	117
Immunity Support	121
The Author	127
The Contributors	129

WELCOME to *Creative Eating – Simple & Healthy Recipes for a Busy Lifestyle!* We are so happy you picked up this book, and we are excited for you as you continue your health journey that will include some of the recipes that follow. Deanna and I have tried many of them whether they have been our own creations, existing recipes we have tweaked or those submitted and created by others we know through social media or personal contacts. We trust you will find many that are tasty to your palate and hope you will also experiment with some that may not be something you would have tried before. We have made every effort possible to give credit for various recipes including the sources and attempted to include a variety of options whether you are vegetarian, vegan or you eat meat/ animal products. Of course, any of the recipes can be changed to your liking. I know I have personally left things out on purpose, or I have left them out because I just didn't have what the recipe called for and was pleasantly surprised in the final product. So…feel free to experiment too!

We want to start off by letting you know that the healthiest version of the recipes in the book can only be so if you stick to organics as much as possible. The following list is a reminder of the produce that seem to have the highest percentages of pesticides that are non-organic so…with that being said, stick to organic for these items.

Buy Organic Only (below)

- Apples
- Peaches
- Nectarines
- Strawberries
- Grapes
- Celery
- Sweet bell peppers
- Snap peas (imported)
- Potatoes (sweet & white)
- Hot peppers
- Kale and collard greens
- Tomatoes
- Spinach
- Cucumbers

Remember to wash all your produce whether it is organic or not in white distilled vinegar and baking soda. Let the produce sit for at least 10 minutes in the water before rinsing well and air drying. The vinegar actually helps keep your produce longer.

Tips from the Author,
Your Personal Lifestyle Coach

A RECIPE FOR SUCCESS

I posted the following question on our Facebook groups, and after hearing the responses which included every single one of these, I decided to add some tips to this recipe book to help those of you on the healthy living journey.

What's the HARDEST part about getting on track with your health and fitness?

   sticking to eating healthier

   getting in my workouts

   finding the time

   feeling overwhelmed with the whole process

> What's the HARDEST part about getting on track with your health and fitness?

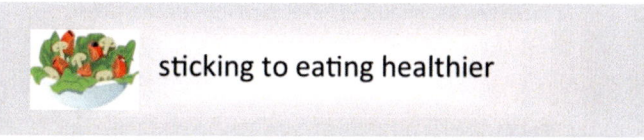

If this is you, here are a few tips:

- Keep good healthy food in your fridge and cupboards and you'll eat healthy food!! Keep the other stuff out of sight – possibly in a cupboard you rarely go to (this is especially important for those of you in households where others are not eating healthy – ask them to put their stuff in non-see-through containers for the fridge or cupboards).

- Get an accountability partner – try to make this person someone you are around a lot so they see what you are doing as well as ask the hard questions of you weekly (or more if needed).

- Shop the exterior aisles of the grocery store and stay away from the middle aisles which are full of junk and processed foods!

- Eat tons of raw fruit and veggies and healthy fats to fill your tummy along with lots of pure water.

- Munch on celery, cucumbers, leafy greens while you are making meals – especially dinner, and especially if that dinner you are making for your family is NOT a healthy one because they are not on board with the changes you are making.

- Always have a baggie of sunflower seeds, pumpkin seeds and a few almonds in your purse, car, and desk drawer.

- Leaving the house to run errands? or going to be out and about for awhile? Take a granny smith apple with you or a small bag of celery and carrots.

- Always plan ahead – look at your calendar at the beginning of the week and check for events where you know unhealthy food will be present (eat before you go or prepare a healthy snack or food item to bring that you can eat and share), or plan for a cheat (it is not a treat, it is a cheat). Indulge and enjoy whatever it may be – a smaller portion than you would have done in the past.

- Don't cheat daily – cheat once a week and then extend that out to longer intervals as you grow and make permanent changes.

- Keep your goal in mind (maybe it is eating 80% clean weekly).

- Commit to our 30-Day Jumpstart challenge – it truly does give you a jumpstart on healthy eating and sticking to self-discipline.

- Limit the number of times you eat out, or don't eat at restaurants at all. If you are going out, check the menu online ahead of time and make up your mind before going what you are going to have.

- Get involved in a community – you need to hang out with like-minded people who are eating healthy as well (if you are not part of the Fit 'n' Faith group, start one; or at least join the one on social media for support!

- Keep a healthy mindset (you are not depriving yourself – you are giving yourself the gift of health and energy by making healthy choices.

- Pray about this a lot! Taking care of your body honors God so keep making better choices.

- When you blow it, don't give in to the temptation to quit or give up – stay in the battle – YOU are worth it!

> **What's the HARDEST part about getting on track with your health and fitness?**

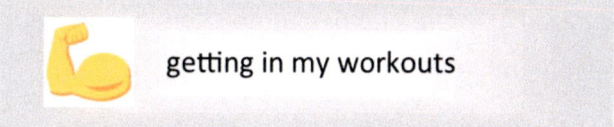

Tips:

- Start out slow – don't over-commit so you can keep your goals – I.e., 1 full hour workout a week, stretch 5 mins a day – and by the way, put it on your calendar, set alarms on your phone, etc. This will help.

- Buddy system works best – have someone do that 1 hour workout with you, and increase as you are able.

- Work toward 30 mins of doing something every day, but again, baby steps – 5 mins a day and 1 day off is good to start along with the 1 hour weekly.

- Try different things. Find something you really, really enjoy and make it fun! Ideas: cardio drumming, stretching classes (like our S&S classes), Pilates, walking, running, Zumba, Jazzercise, rebounding – find a place that will let you come and try a class FREE or with a minimum cost.

- Everyone is different. The timing of your workouts is critical. What works for me may not work for you. Many people promote a first thing in the morning type of workout. That is definitely not me. Find what works for you and stick with it. I know individuals that actually work out in the middle of the day (simple stretches can be done anywhere) and some that work out immediately after work. I think that is a good way to do it if you plan to work out in the evening. Do not go home. If you go home, the risk of staying home is too great. Instead, take a snack with you to work to eat before your workout, and take your workout clothes with you to work so you are able to go immediately after you finish your work day.

- Keep in mind your workouts don't have to be at a gym or in a class. I encourage you to take at least one class per week if possible but if you cannot, no worries! You will need extra accountability and encouragement to complete workouts at home because it is so easy to be distracted and fill your time with other things. But, working out at home can be very comfortable, and you have greater flexibility of time. You can still use the buddy system even though your buddy is working out at their house and not with you.

- To work out at home, invest in some exercise bands or small weights and an exercise mat to use – that will probably be all you need. Be sure to incorporate stretching, strength training and some cardio each week if possible. The cardio can be as simple as doing the surge workouts for a couple of minutes which is described in our *Fit 'n' Faith* book or you can find information online.

- Have physical limitations? Check out Pinterest for chair exercises. They are great!

➤ **What's the HARDEST part about getting on track with your health and fitness?**

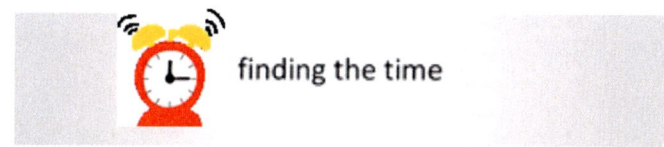

For those who responded that this is an issue:

- Just a reminder – We make time for the things that we value and are important. If you are having difficulty finding the time, then perhaps you need to investigate why you do not value what needs to change.

- Here is an assignment for you: take a pad of paper and write down how you spend every single minute of each day; how much time you sleep, how much time you spend eating, how much time you're on social media, emails, phone calls, texts, reading, randomly sitting – and how about sitting in front of the television set? – spending time with friends, going to restaurants / eating out, vacationing, etc. Every single minute; write it down. I believe that this exercise is very telling as it relates to finding the time. Evaluate all that you have written and begin to look at the things that can be adjusted. You must have a schedule and a routine in place so you take care of you! Taking care of you as it relates to this topic means finding the time for the exercise and finding time to make meals or a green smoothie. Again, this means prioritizing your health and well-being over some of the superficial things that you are engaging in on a regular basis.

- The majority of us have a very busy schedule. And as we look over our schedule, it seems like nothing can be cut. If you find yourself in this situation, there are ways that we can simplify this journey. 1) we mentioned the different forms of exercise that you can do that do not take as long as others. 2) Food preparation – I recommend finding recipes that are healthy that have limited ingredients and very limited preparation. I would also recommend cooking large batches of food that can be warmed up as leftovers or frozen and taken out of the freezer at random which will save you time as well. These are some of the things that I have found very helpful in our busy lives. This is the whole foundation for putting this recipe book together – simple, quick, delicious and healthy.

> **What's the HARDEST part about getting on track with your health and fitness?**

 feeling overwhelmed with the whole process

For those who responded that this is an issue:

- I bet you have heard this: "How do you eat an elephant?" (Not that we should ever consider eating one – LOL) The answer is: "One bite at a time." This is why we developed the baby step program in the *Fit 'n' Faith* book. None of us can tackle a lot of change all at once. If we try to, we will 99.9% of the time, fail. :-(So... take a deep breath and spend some time evaluating where to begin.

- If you do not have access to our Baby Step Program, I encourage you to get the book *Fit 'n' Faith* – it will help you tremendously.

- Where to begin? If you do not follow the Baby Step Program, here is another way to start: Prioritize! What are the majors (most important and obvious changes that need to be made) in your life right now? Focus there and not on the minors – you will get to those down the road.

- So what's a major? Consider your current health condition. What are the things bothering you the most? Ideas: weight – hard to get around / breathe?, illness – keep getting sick or have been diagnosed with a disease?, toxins – feel like you are dragging and exhausted from your environment?, under conviction of the Holy Spirit – time to practice obedience and wrestle through the discomfort of leaving an addiction behind? These and others you ask yourself are all questions that might be helpful in determining what your priority should be. Now that you have it… get started! One step at a time, one day at a time!

- I want to remind you again of this truth: trying to tackle this alone will always feel overwhelming! If it is a shared burden with others on the journey with you, the weight is lifted. We need encouragement, accountability, support and prayers!

- Set some "manageable (be realistic) goals." Where do you want to be and what do you want to accomplish in the next month? E.g., by the end of the month I want to be completely off sugar and fast food, increase my water intake by _____, eat meat only 3 x's a week, have all new non-toxic cleaning products, be stretching 5 minutes per day, be taking a Sabbath or at least a ½ day Sabbath, find a weekly class / group I can participate in, have an accountability partner, etc.

- At the end of every day, take the time to review the changes you have made for that day and celebrate – be thankful!! And remember, tomorrow is another day – new habits will be created over time. You've got this!

CREATIVE EATING

SMOOTHIES

Smoothie options to try: Eliminate the stevia or sweetener on any that call for that for the 30-Day Program, and even try to leave out things that you might not have on hand, and just try them.

Super Charged Key Lime Pie Smoothie

Serves: 1

INGREDIENTS

- 2 cups full-fat organic coconut milk
- ½ cup soaked cashews
- 2 Tbsp of raw honey
- ½ avocado
- 1 large handful of spinach
- juice of one lime
- 1 frozen banana
- ¼ tsp vanilla

Detox Drink (eliminate stevia for 30-Day Program)

Total Time: 2 minutes   Serves: 1

INGREDIENTS

- 1 glass of filtered water (12-16 oz.)
- 2 Tbsp lemon juice
- 1 dash Cayenne Pepper (optional)
- 2 Tbsp apple cider vinegar
- 1 tsp cinnamon
- stevia to taste

Instructions:

Blend all ingredients together.

Choc-Banana Smoothie Bowl

The combination of cacao, coconut and maca makes this the perfect mood-boosting and hormone-balancing bowl of goodness. Plus, it tastes just like a bowl of chocolate and banana ice cream, so why wouldn't you be happier after eating this?

INGREDIENTS

- 1 frozen banana
- 1 Tbsp cacao powder
- 1 Tbsp coconut oil
- 1 tsp vanilla
- 1 tsp chia seeds
- ½ cup coconut milk
- 1 Tbsp shredded coconut
- ½ Tbsp maca powder
- 1 tsp cinnamon
- 2 dates (pitted)

Instructions:

Blend everything together in your blender and enjoy this one in a bowl, just like you are enjoying a bowl of ice cream...only 10 times better!

The Green Mood Booster

INGREDIENTS

- 1 frozen banana
- ½ avocado
- 1 tsp vanilla
- ½ cup coconut water
- 1 handful of greens (e.g., spinach, kale)
- 2 Tbsp nut butter
- 1 cup almond milk
- 3 Tbsp raw cacao nibs

Instructions:

Blend everything (except raw cacao nibs). Once the smoothie is nice and smooth, add in cacao nibs and give another blend. We like to still have a little crunch in these, and it's nice to sprinkle some on top! Enjoy.

Don't let those cravings win you over with chocolate and sweets, use these cravings as an excuse to make a beautiful berry smoothie like this one. The addition of cacao powder will give you an extra boost of happiness while also feeding your chocolate craving.

Berry-Rich Craving Saver

INGREDIENTS

- ½ cup blueberries
- 1 cup coconut milk
- 3-5 strawberries, depending on size and freshness
- ½ avocado
- 1 Tbsp goji berries
- 1 Tbsp cacao powder (optional)
- 2 tsp ground flaxseed
- 1 tsp chia seeds

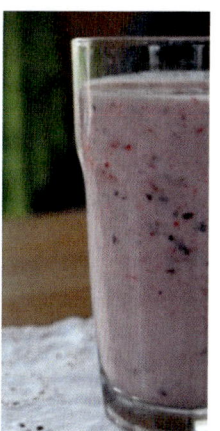

Instructions:
Blend everything together until totally smooth and enjoy!

Carrot Mango Coconut

INGREDIENTS

- 1 large carrot (grated)
- 1 cup frozen mango
- 1-2 Tbsp unsweetened shredded coconut

Instructions:
Blend with ½ to 1 cup liquid.

Cherry Blueberry Kale

- 1 cup kale
- 1 cup cherries
- ½ cup blueberries

Instructions:
Blend with ½ to 1 cup liquid.

Chocolate Banana Nut Smoothie Recipe

Total Time: 2 minutes   Serves: 1

INGREDIENTS

- 1 cup coconut milk
- 1 banana, peeled
- 2 cups ice cubes
- ⅓ cup sprouted almond butter
- 2 Tbsp cacao powder
- stevia to taste

Directions:

Place all ingredients in a blender and blend until desired consistency is reached. Serve immediately.

One of the easiest ways to give your day a swift nutritional kick first thing in the morning? Sipping down a smoothie. Whether you're breaking your cleanse or just keeping your body strong, there is a smoothie concoction perfect for every morning.

Pumpkin Coconut Paleo Smoothie Recipe

INGREDIENTS

- 1 cup pumpkin purée (organic or make your own from scratch is best)
- 1 cup coconut milk (full fat, not light)
- 1 frozen banana
- 2 Tbsp almond butter
- cinnamon

Instructions:

Place all ingredients in the blender and blend until smooth. Serves: 2

Cherry Mango Yogurt

- 1 cup diced mango
- ½ cup plain unsweetened yogurt
- 1 cup frozen cherries

Instructions:

Blend with ½ to 1 cup liquid.

Ginger Pina Colada

    2 cups frozen pineapple   **1 lime (peeled and sliced)**
    ½ inch piece of ginger (thinly sliced)

Instructions:
Blend with ½ to 1 cup liquid.

Raspberry Banana Chia

    1 ½ cups frozen raspberries
    1 large banana (sliced)
    1 Tbsp chia seeds

Instructions:
Blend with ½ to 1 cup liquid.

Cranberry Pineapple Spinach

    1 ½ cups pineapple   **½ cup cranberries**
    1 cup spinach

Instructions:
Blend with ½ to 1 cup liquid. (Can substitute another berry for the cranberries.)

Banana Blueberry Chocolate

    1 large banana (sliced)
    1 cup blueberries
    1 Tbsp cocoa or cacao powder

Instructions:
Blend with ½ to 1 cup liquid.

Tangerine Pineapple Banana

    2 tangerines (peeled and segmented)   **½ cup frozen pineapple**
    1 frozen banana

Instructions:
Blend with ½ to 1 cup liquid.

Peanut Butter Strawberry

    1 cup frozen strawberries   **1 large banana (sliced)**
    1-2 Tbsp peanut butter

Instructions:
Blend with ½ to 1 cup liquid.

Mango Berry Coconut

    1 cup mixed berries   **1 cup mango**
    2 Tbsp unsweetened shredded coconut

Instructions:
Blend with ½ to 1 cup liquid.

Green Swiss Chard Smoothie

by Jim Perko, YouBeauty Culinary Expert   Servings: 5

INGREDIENTS

    2 cups cleaned swiss chard, stems removed, leaves roughly chopped, firmly packed
    1 Bartlett pear, core, stem and seeds removed
    1 cup green seedless grapes   **1 orange, peeled and quartered**
    2 bananas, peeled   **1 tsp chia seeds**
    ¼ cup water   **2 cups ice**

Kale, Pineapple and Coconut Milk Smoothie

by Heather Bauer, R.D.   Servings: 2

INGREDIENTS

- **1 scoop Vanilla Whey Protein Powder (use a plant-based powder for 30-Day)**
- **½ cup unsweetened coconut milk or coconut water**
- **2 cups baby kale or baby spinach**
- **1 ½ cups chopped pineapple**
- **1 ripe banana, frozen, broken into chunks**
- **ice**

Apple, Peanut Butter and Chocolate Power Smoothie

by the Pretty Life Girls

INGREDIENTS

- **1 cup unsweetened almond milk**
- **2 Tbsp peanut powder**
- **½ medium apple with peel**
- **1 scoop chocolate protein powder**
- **½ banana**
- **¾ cup ice**

Instructions:

Place all ingredients into blender and blend on high to desired consistency. Serve immediately and enjoy!

Chocolate/ Peanut Smoothie

- coconut milk
- spinach
- celery
- 2 dates pitted
- 1 Tbsp coconut oil
- 1 Tbsp peanut powder
- ice
- purified water
- carrots
- banana
- 1 Tbsp milled flaxseed
- 2 Tbsp cocoa powder
- 1 scoop of pea protein

Berry Protein Bash

Serves: 2

This is one of our favorite combos – strawberries, blueberries and banana. We up the protein by adding almonds. We also love the extra dietary fiber and vitamin E from the almonds.

INGREDIENTS

- 2 cups spinach, fresh
- 1 cup strawberries
- 1 banana
- 2 cups almond milk, unsweetened
- 1 cup blueberries
- ½ cup almonds*

Directions:

Blend spinach and almond milk until smooth.

Next add the remaining fruits and blend again.

*Soak almonds overnight in water before blending, or use almond meal instead. Use at least one frozen fruit to make the green smoothie cold. Any variety of berry can be substituted.

Immunity Green Smoothie

by Katrine van Wyk, author of "Best Green Drinks Ever"   Serves: 1

INGREDIENTS

- 1 cup coconut water
- 2 leaves romaine lettuce
- ½ green apple, such as Granny Smith
- ¼ cucumber
- ¼ avocado, peeled
- ½ lemon, peeled
- ½-inch slice fresh ginger
- ½ cup fresh parsley
- 1 serving probiotic powder or the contents of a probiotic capsule
    (follow instructions on the bottle)
- 3-4 ice cubes, optional

SMOOTHIES   23

Vanilla Cinnamon Smoothie

coconut milk	purified water
spinach	carrots
celery	banana
one pitted date	½ tsp vanilla
½ scoop of pea protein	milled flaxseed
1 Tbsp coconut oil	1 tsp cinnamon
ice	

Frozen Green Lemonade

by Katrine van Wyk, author of "Best Green Drinks Ever"   Serves: 1

INGREDIENTS

½ cup chilled mint tea	½ cup spinach
½ cup or 2 leaves romaine lettuce	5 mint leaves
1 lemon, peeled	5 drops or 1 packet Stevia
1 cup ice	

Strawberry Lime Smoothie

by Kelly H, Ypsilanti MI

1 cup coconut milk	handful of cashews
10 medium fresh or frozen strawberries	¼ tsp vanilla
1 tsp lime juice or 1 drop of lime oil	dash of cinnamon
1 tsp coconut oil	dash of salt
honey or monk fruit extract to taste	ice
½ banana (I used frozen)	
filtered water if needed	

Makes about 16 oz. (2 cups)

Nut Butter Chocolate

    1 ½ cups almond milk (unsweetened)

    ½ Tbsp cacao powder

    ½ Tbsp almond butter

    banana

    cinnamon

    vanilla protein powder

*You could add **coconut oil** or **flax seeds** if you want.

Strawberry Orange Smoothie

    1 cup baby spinach

    ½ cup carrot

    1 scoop protein powder

    ½ cup almond milk (unsweetened)

    1 orange (peeled)

    1 Tbsp milled flaxseed

    3 frozen strawberries

    ¼ cup filtered water

Consistency via blender: medium

Makes 16 oz. (2 cups) blended

Chocolate Cherry Green Smoothie

by Dreamy Leaf

    1 cup plant or nut milk

    3 Tbsp raw cacao

    1 cup (or more) pitted cherries - you can use frozen

    3 Tbsp hemp seeds, optional for extra protein and healthy fats

    ½ avocado (can sub ½ frozen banana)

    1 big handful of spinach

    1 Tbsp chia seeds

    dash of cinnamon

Throw all ingredients in a high power blender and blend until smooth.

*For a sweeter smoothie, add in a pitted Medjool date.

Tropical Smoothie

by Kelly H, Ypsilanti MI

- almond milk or coconut milk
- fresh or frozen mango
- lots of fresh spinach
- vanilla extract
- supergreens powder
- Fiji or filtered water
- pure pineapple juice
- unsweetened shredded coconut
- monk fruit extract to preferred sweetness
- several almonds and a few Brazil nuts
- pineapple coconut electrolytes

Experiment with proportions.

Banana Split Smoothie

by Sherry P, Tiffanie C & Renee M (Fit 'n' Faith weekend)

This recipe makes plenty to share.

- 1 cup almond milk
- 4 strawberries
- 2 cups spinach
- about a ¼ tsp Cayenne pepper
- 2 Tbsp hemp seeds
- 1 scoop vanilla pea protein
- lots of ice
- ½ - 1 cup filtered water
- 2 bananas
- 2 Tbsp cacao powder
- 2-3 Tbsp coconut oil
- 3 Tbsp chia seeds
- 1 packet monk fruit sweetener

Fruity Green Smoothie

by Sandy M & Brenda M (Fit 'n' Faith weekend)

- 1 cup almond milk
- 1 apricot
- 1 large apple
- 2 tsp hemp seeds
- 1 ½ scoops protein powder
- 2 handfuls of spinach
- 1 small banana
- 1 tsp coconut oil
- 2 tsp chia seeds
- ¾ - 1 cup ice

Blend and enjoy.

Juice – Great Juice to create with your juicer if you have one!
- ginger
- kale
- carrots
- kiwi
- lemon
- 2 green apples
- half a zucchini
- orange

Coffee Creamer
- Kerry Gold brand butter (which is organic grass fed)
- organic coffee grounds
- cinnamon
- a small amount of honey

Turmeric Coffee
INGREDIENTS
- 2 cups organic coffee
- ¼ tsp turmeric
- ¼ tsp cinnamon
- 1 tsp of XCT oil (MCT oil or coconut oil works as well)
- 1 tsp of butter (organic from grass fed cows of course)
- Dash of sea salt
- 1 squirt each of Vanilla Stevia and English Toffee Stevia (or a sweetener and/or flavor of your choice)

Instructions:
Brew 2 cups of coffee and pour into a glass blender while it's still hot. Add all other ingredients and blend. Serve and enjoy! Makes 2 cups of coffee.

SALADS

Pear & Walnuts Salad (add turkey or chicken if desired)

Serves: approx. 6

DRESSING INGREDIENTS
- 1 Tbsp choice of mustard
- 1 Tbsp apple cider vinegar
- ¼ cup olive oil
- sea salt & pepper

SALAD INGREDIENTS
- 1 - 5oz bag of mixed greens
- 2 Bartlett pears, thinly sliced
- 8 oz of cubed or sliced turkey breast (or eliminate meat altogether)
- 4 oz of cubed Gouda cheese (I use a vegan alternative)
- 2/3 cup walnuts
- ¼ cup dried cranberries

Blackbean Lime Salad

By Megan M., Plymouth MI

INGREDIENTS
- black beans
- cucumber
- tomato
- lime juice
- chickpeas
- corn
- avocado
- sea salt and pepper

Easy Citrus Salad

INGREDIENTS
- spinach
- kale
- strawberries
- grapes
- almonds

DRESSING INGREDIENTS
- grapeseed oil
- apple cider vinegar
- fresh squeezed lemon juice or lemon oil (must be ingestible)
- fresh squeezed orange juice or orange oil (must be ingestible)

Fruity Green Salad

INGREDIENTS
- spinach
- kale (optional)
- mushrooms
- zucchini
- half an avocado
- kiwi
- mango
- berries (blueberries, raspberries, strawberries, whatever you like)

*For fewer calories, you don't have to add so much fruit. Also, you can add nuts.

DRESSING INGREDIENTS
- ¼ cup grape seed oil
- ¼ cup apple cider vinegar
- lemon oil or juice
- orange oil or juice

SALADS 29

Chickpea Salad

Prep Time: 10 minutes   Total Time: 10 minutes
by Holly N.   Serves: 6

SALAD INGREDIENTS

- **1 avocado**
- **1 can chickpeas, drained (19 oz)**
- **2 cups grape tomatoes, sliced**
- **½ cup fresh parsley**
- **½ fresh lemon**
- **¼ cup sliced red onion**
- **2 cups diced cucumber**
- **¾ cup diced green bell pepper**

DRESSING INGREDIENTS

- **¼ cup olive oil**
- **½ tsp cumin**
- **salt and pepper**
- **2 Tbsp apple cider vinegar**
- **Italian spice mix**

Instructions:

Cut avocado into cubes and place in bowl. Squeeze the juice from ½ lemon over the avocado and gently stir to combine.

Add remaining salad ingredients and gently toss to combine.

Refrigerate at least one hour before serving.

Variations: Add cooked black beans, maybe some cilantro, onions

Cinnamon, Apple, Walnut, Kale and Quinoa Salad

by Sara Wylie   Serves: 6

INGREDIENTS

⅔ cup dry or 2 cups cooked quinoa

3 large handfuls kale, stalks removed and finely chopped

3 medium apples, cored and diced (use sweet variety)

5 celery stalks, diced

1 cup walnut halves or pieces

CINNAMON DRESSING

¼ cup extra virgin olive oil

¼ cup apple cider vinegar

2 Tbsp maple syrup or honey

½ lemon (the juice)

1 tsp cinnamon

1 tsp salt

½ tsp ground black pepper

Instructions:
- Cook dry quinoa according to package instructions. If using leftover quinoa, measure 2 cups. Add to a large mixing bowl along with kale, walnuts, apples and celery.
- In a small skillet, toast walnuts on low-medium heat until lightly brown, about 5 minutes. Stir frequently and watch closely not to burn. Transfer to a bowl with other ingredients.
- In a small bowl, whisk together Cinnamon Dressing ingredients, pour over salad and stir gently. Serve cold or warm, on its own or with chicken or turkey.

Notes/Storage Instructions:

Refrigerate salad without the dressing for up to 2 days. Dressing keeps well refrigerated for a few weeks. All dressed salad stays fresh in the fridge for up to 1 day.

Harvest Cobb Salad

by Sara Wylie   Total Time: 30 mins   Serves: 4

INGREDIENTS

- 2 large eggs
- 1 apple, diced
- ½ cup pecan halves
- ⅓ cup crumbled goat cheese
- 6 cups chopped romaine lettuce
- 1 pear, diced
- ⅓ cup dried cranberries

POPPY SEED DRESSING

- ⅓ cup mayonnaise (or substitute)
- ¼ cup milk (or any plant milk option)
- 1 Tbsp raw honey
- 1 Tbsp apple cider vinegar
- 1 Tbsp poppy seeds

Instructions:

- To make the poppy seed dressing, whisk together mayonnaise, milk, honey, apple cider vinegar and poppy seeds in a small bowl; set aside.
- Place eggs in a large saucepan and cover with cold water by 1 inch. Bring to a boil and cook for 1 minute. Cover eggs with a tight-fitting lid and remove from heat; set aside for 8-10 minutes. Drain well and let cool before peeling and dicing.
- To assemble the salad, place romaine lettuce in a large bowl; top with arranged rows of eggs, apple, pear, pecans, cranberries and goat cheese.
- Serve immediately with poppy seed dressing.

Salad with Chickpeas

INGREDIENTS

    Romaine lettuce   **spinach**

    cucumbers   **tomatoes**

    green onions   **sea salt**

    extra virgin olive oil   **ginger root**

    lemon (squeezed)   **vinegar**

    no-sugar dried raspberries   **chickpeas**

Instructions:
Combine all ingredients. Took me 15 minutes.

Apple, Pecan and Feta Salad

Prep Time: 15 mins   Total Time: 30 mins

by Sara Wylie   Serves: 1 big salad

SALAD INGREDIENTS

    3 cups kale, de-stemmed, washed and torn

    1 apple, sliced thinly

    2 Tbsp cranberries

    2 Tbsp pecans

    3 Tbsp feta cheese, crumbled

HONEY-APPLE VINAIGRETTE DRESSING INGREDIENTS

    1 Tbsp honey

    1 Tbsp apple cider vinegar

    2 Tbsp olive oil

    ½ tsp salt

    ½ tsp ground black pepper

Instructions:
- In a bowl, place the kale. Add the apples, cranberries, pecans and feta cheese on top – if you'd like, toss them in a bowl first then sprinkle on top.
- Whisk the dressing together and pour over the salad.
- Enjoy!

Sweet and Salty Fall Harvest Salad

by Sara Wylie   Prep Time: 1 hour   Serves: 4

SALAD INGREDIENTS

    1 large butternut squash, peeled, seeded and cubed
    3 Tbsp extra virgin olive oil, divided
    sea salt and freshly ground black pepper
    ½ cup chopped pecans
    1 Tbsp unsalted butter
    2 + Tbsp of chosen sweetener
       (or brown sugar substitute)
    1 bunch of kale, washed, stems removed,
       and roughly chopped (about 8 cups)
    6 oz brie, cubed
    1 large apple, cored and roughly chopped
    ½ cup dried cranberries

MAPLE VINAIGRETTE INGREDIENTS

    2 Tbsp pure maple syrup
    up to ⅓ cup extra virgin olive oil
    1 tsp Dijon mustard (or substitute)
    1 Tbsp apple cider vinegar
    ¾ tsp sea salt

Instructions:

- Preheat oven to 425°F. Spread the squash out on a large baking sheet and drizzle with 2 Tbsp of olive oil, then sprinkle with some salt and pepper. Roast for 35 minutes, toss the squash and roast for another 15 to 20 minutes, tossing periodically until the squash is browned and softened.
- While the squash roasts, make the candied pecan clusters. Ready a Silpat or line a baking sheet with parchment paper; set aside. Heat the butter and brown sugar substitute over medium heat in a medium nonstick pan until bubbling. Toss the pecans into the butter-sugar mixture until coated. Cook, stirring occasionally, until the sugar liquefies and turns a dark amber color. Pour the pecans out onto the Silpat or parchment paper and spread them out with a rubber spatula. Allow them to cool

completely before breaking them up into clusters.
- Make the vinaigrette: Whisk the maple syrup, ¼ cup olive oil, mustard, vinegar and salt together in a medium bowl or shake it all together in a mason jar. Whisk in additional olive oil in small increments up to ⅓ cup total until you reach your desired dressing consistency.
- In a large bowl, toss the kale with the remaining 1 Tbsp of olive oil. Massage the oil into the kale with your hands until the kale turns bright green and glossy, about 2-3 minutes.
- Top the kale with the squash, brie, apples, cranberries and pecan clusters. Drizzle the maple vinaigrette over the top of the salad before serving while the squash is still warm.

Tabouli

by Kelly H, Ypsilanti MI

INGREDIENTS

    1 cup (or less) medium burghul (wheat) OR substitute quinoa
    2 bunches fresh parsley (about 4 cups), remove leaves from thicker stems
    1 bunch fresh mint (about 2 cups), remove leaves from stems
    3 bunches green onions (the thinner the better), use the white AND green parts
    3-4 average tomatoes, finely diced
    juice from 3-4 fresh lemons (about ¾ cup)
    ¼ cup extra virgin olive oil
    sea salt and black pepper to taste

Instructions:

Chop fine the parsley, mint, onions and tomatoes. If desired, a food processor may be used to chop the parsley and mint. Mix all the ingredients well in a large bowl. Adjust seasoning, lemon juice, and olive oil to taste.

SALADS

Quinoa Tabouli

I like to divide this into ½ cup - 1 cup portions. Excellent for Food Prepping or Lunches on-the-go as it's delicious served cold or at room temperature.

INGREDIENTS
- 3 cups cooked quinoa
- 4-5 small tomatoes, diced
- 1 small red onion, diced
- 3-4 medium cucumbers, peeled and diced
- 1 cup roughly chopped fresh parsley
- juice from 3-4 fresh lemons
- 1–1 ½ Tbsp avocado oil or extra virgin olive oil to taste
- sea salt, black pepper

Instructions:
Place everything in a large bowl and combine. Adjust seasoning, lemon juice, and olive oil to taste.

Cucumber Salad

INGREDIENTS
- 4 medium cucumbers, seedless if desired
- 1 oz of minced onion
- 3-4 oz of Vegenaise
- juice of one lemon
- 1 Tbsp sea salt
- ¼ cup of chopped fresh dill
- ¼ tsp black pepper

Instructions:
1. Trim off ends of cucumbers and peel alternate stripes on them (or peel completely, or just leave the peel on like I do).
2. Slice thin and toss in bowl with salt; allow to cure for 10-12 minutes.
3. Rinse off salt thoroughly, allow to drain.
4. Add onion, dill and black pepper, then add lemon juice (more can be added if desired)
5. Add Vegenaise and adjust creaminess as desired.

Fall Harvest Salad with Maple Vinaigrette

INGREDIENTS

- 1 (14-ounce) can kidney beans, drained, rinsed
- ½ pomegranate, arils removed
- 6 ounces goat cheese, crumbled
- 2 Granny Smith apples, diced
- 4 celery stalks, diced
- ½ red onion, diced
- 2 cups spinach, chopped
- ¾ cup pecans, toasted
- ¾ cup raisins
- 1 cucumber, peeled, diced

INGREDIENTS FOR THE MAPLE VINAIGRETTE

- ¼ cup olive oil
- ½ Tbsp balsamic vinegar
- 2 Tbsp maple syrup
- 1 tsp lemon juice
- salt, to taste
- pepper, to taste

Instructions:

In a large bowl, toss together all salad ingredients.

In a separate bowl, whisk together vinaigrette ingredients. Taste and adjust to your liking (add more maple syrup for additional sweetness).

Chill each separately in the fridge. Drizzle vinaigrette over salad just before serving.

SALADS 37

Sesame Kale Salad

Serves: 3   Prep Time: 5 min   Cook Time: 15 min   Total Time: 20 min

INGREDIENTS

- **1 cup quinoa**
- **1 Tbsp coconut oil/sesame oil**
- **½ of a red onion**
- **1 clove garlic, minced**
- **3 cups kale, de-stemmed and torn**
- **2 cups broccoli florets (about 1 small head)**
- **2 Tbsp coconut aminos (similar to soy sauce)**
- **2 Tbsp water**
- **juice from ½ - 1 lime, depending on your liking**
- **½ Tbsp Dijon mustard**
- **1 tsp fresh ginger, minced (or powdered)**
- **½ tsp black pepper**
- **dash of red pepper flakes (optional)**
- **2 Tbsp sesame seeds (black or white) – you could also use any other seed you like**

Instructions:

- Combine 1 cup quinoa with 2 cups water in a medium-sized pot. Bring to a boil and reduce heat to simmer for about 15 minutes or until all water has been absorbed.
- Meanwhile, in a small saucepan, melt the coconut oil on medium-high heat. Add the red onion and sauté for 2-3 minutes. Add the garlic, kale, broccoli. Sauté for about 3 minutes.
- In a small bowl, combine the water, lime juice, Dijon mustard, ginger, pepper, red pepper flakes and seeds. Add mixture to saucepan with vegetables and mix until well combined. Cook for about 2 more minutes.
- Once quinoa is finished cooking, scoop it into 2-3 bowls and top with the vegetable mixture. Add extra coconut aminos as needed.

Mexican Salad Dressing

This is a great and easy salad dressing for Mexican inspired dishes. Great on tacos and burritos too!

Makes about 10 Tablespoons of dressing.   Serving Size: 1 Tablespoon

by SparkPeople user KIMBERLEIGH06

INGREDIENTS

- ½ avocado
- ¼ tsp minced garlic
- ¼ tsp fresh ground black pepper
- juice of one wedge of lime
- ½ cup unsweetened nut milk
- ¼ tsp sea salt
- ¼ tsp chili powder

Instructions:

Place all ingredients in a food processor or blender and pulse until everything is creamy.

Quinoa Salad

INGREDIENTS (use any quantities of the ingredients that you desire)

- quinoa
- cucumber
- tomato
- zucchini
- onion
- celery
- cilantro

DRESSING INGREDIENTS

- **olive oil**
- **Italian spice**
- **apple cider vinegar**

Instructions:

Cook Quinoa, then cool.

Dice up the cucumber, tomato, zucchini, onion, celery and cilantro. Add to quinoa.

For the dressing, mix together the olive oil, Italian spice and apple cider vinegar.

Loaded Lentil Salad

Prep Time: 15 mins   Cook Time: 20 mins   Total Time: 35 mins
by Alexis, sponsored by Hello Fresh   Serves: 4

This hearty Loaded Lentil Salad is packed with protein, fiber, and warm veggies like roasted sweet potatoes, red onion, and Brussels sprouts. Perfect for a light lunch! Vegan and gluten-free.

INGREDIENTS
- 3 medium sweet potatoes, diced into ½ inch cubes
- 2 tsp Herbs de Provence
- 2 tsp pure maple syrup or honey
- ¼ cup extra virgin olive oil, divided
- 2 red onions, diced
- 16oz Brussels sprouts, thinly sliced
- 1 cup French lentils
- 3 cups water
- ¼ cup balsamic vinegar
- ⅓ cup pepitas
- ½ tsp salt + pepper to taste

Instructions:
- Preheat oven to 425°F. Line a baking sheet with foil or parchment paper.
- Combine sweet potatoes, Herbs de Provence, maple syrup or honey, 1 Tbsp olive oil, and a pinch of salt in a medium boil. Spread onto prepared baking sheet and roast for about 11-13 minutes. Toss and roast until golden, another 11-13 minutes.
- Heat ½ Tbsp olive oil in a medium pot over medium heat. Add onion and cook until softened, about 5 minutes. Add lentils and water. Bring to a boil then reduce heat to low and simmer until tender, about 15-20 minutes. Season with another pinch of salt and drain any excess water. Return to pot.
- Heat ½ Tbsp olive oil in a medium pan over medium heat. Add Brussels sprouts and cook until golden brown, 4-5 minutes. Season with salt and pepper to taste.
- Add balsamic vinegar and remaining 2 Tbsp olive oil to pot with lentils. Add Brussels sprouts, roasted sweet potatoes, and salt and pepper to taste. Top with pepitas and serve!

Shaved Root Salad with Crispy Lentils

Serves: 6   Ready in 1 Hour

DRESSING INGREDIENTS

- 2 Tbsp extra virgin olive oil
- 1 Tbsp mustard
- 1 Tbsp apple cider vinegar
- 1 clove garlic, grated
- 1 Tbsp pure maple syrup
- 1 Tbsp filtered water
- 1 tsp prepared horseradish
- salt and pepper, to taste

SALAD INGREDIENTS

- ⅓ cup French or black beluga lentils, rinsed
- ½ tsp extra virgin olive oil
- salt and pepper, to taste
- 2 small beets, peeled, or 1 medium
- 2 medium carrots, peeled
- 1 small celery root, peeled
- 2 Tbsp chopped fresh dill (about 2 sprigs), for garnish

Instructions:

- Preheat oven to 400°F.
- Make the dressing: In jar with tight-fitting lid, combine olive oils, maple syrup, mustard, water, vinegar, horseradish, garlic, salt and pepper. Tightly secure lid, and shake jar vigorously until dressing has a creamy and smooth consistency. Set aside.
- Make the salad: Bring medium saucepan of water to a boil. Drop in lentils and a big pinch of salt. Bring to a boil again, and then reduce heat to a simmer until lentils are just tender, about 20 mins. Drain lentils and spread out on kitchen towel to dry.
  Transfer dried lentils to baking sheet. Toss lentils with olive oil, salt and pepper. Slide baking sheet into preheated oven, and roast until lentils have dried and browned slightly, about 8 mins. Remove from oven and set aside.
  Slice beets paper thin and place in large bowl. Slice carrots and add to bowl. Cut celery root down the middle lengthwise. Slice each half of celery root with the mandoline, and add slices to bowl.
  Season all sliced vegetables with salt and pepper, and toss.

Toss sliced vegetables with 2/3 of the dressing. Transfer dressed vegetables to a serving platter. Scatter crispy lentils over vegetables. Pour remaining dressing over lentils. Garnish salad with fresh dill, and serve immediately.

Spinach and Apple Salad with Lemon Dressing

SALAD INGREDIENTS

- 6 cups fresh baby spinach
- 1 apple, thinly sliced
- ½ cup thinly sliced onion

DRESSING INGREDIENTS

- 1/3 cup squeezed lemon juice OR several drops of lemon oil in purified water
- 2 tsp Dijon mustard
- 2 tsp honey
- ½ tsp sea salt
- ½ tsp black pepper
- 2 tsp minced garlic
- 2 Tbsp extra virgin olive oil

Instructions:

Whisk together the lemon juice (or purified water with several drops of lemon oil), mustard, honey, salt, pepper, garlic and olive oil. Drizzle over salad and enjoy!

MAIN DISHES

Mexican Bowl

INGREDIENTS

- 1 can black beans (add some Mung beans if you want and cook from scratch with dried beans)
- 1 package organic taco seasoning (divided; add ½ package to beans)
- 1 small pkg of frozen organic corn
- chickpeas
- cooked quinoa
- sea salt and pepper
- salsa
- vegan cheese

Instructions:

Preheat oven to 350°.

Mix ½ package taco seasoning with black beans. Separately place each ingredient in a circle in a deep baking dish. Sprinkle with salt, pepper and the remainder of the taco seasoning.

Add several scoops of salsa to the center.

Sprinkle vegan cheese on the beans and quinoa (or you can put the vegan cheese over everything).

Warm in the oven until cheese melts.

Enjoy this over a bed of lettuce and add some avocado or guacamole…and don't forget some healthy tortilla chips!

Naked Burritos

By Kelly H, Ypsilanti MI

INGREDIENTS to Sauté
- grapeseed oil (or any healthy oil such as avocado oil or coconut oil)
- onions, sliced
- green pepper (optional: red and yellow pepper too), sliced
- optional: mushrooms
- optional: zucchini, sliced
- optional: spinach (raw or frozen)

ALL OTHER INGREDIENTS
- organic rice (brown, basmati or jasmine) OR quinoa or a quinoa/rice blend, cooked
- organic cheddar, Monterey Jack or Mexican blend cheese OR vegan cheese
- canned black beans, heated (opt: add cilantro & lime or a drop of lime essential oil)
- organic sour cream OR vegan substitute OR plain Greek yogurt
- guacamole
- salsa of your choice
- Trader Joe's corn salsa
- cilantro
- lime
- organic chicken, cooked and seasoned with desired spices (I like rosemary & garlic)

Instructions:

Sauté onions, peppers (and if desired, mushrooms, zucchini and spinach) in oil. When veggies are tender but still brightly colored, remove from heat.

Spoon desired amount of cooked rice or quinoa into a bowl. Layer with sautéed mixture, cheese, black beans, and as much of the list of ingredients as you desire. Enjoy.

Rosemary Garlic Stir Fry

by Kelly H, Ypsilanti MI

INGREDIENTS

- 1 Tbsp grapeseed oil
- 1 medium onion, sliced
- 1 tsp minced garlic
- ¼ tsp dried rosemary
- 1 handful of organic baby carrots OR 2 large carrots, peeled and sliced
- 1 handful of mushrooms, sliced or halved
- ¼ of a yellow pepper, sliced
- ¼ of a red pepper, sliced
- 2 large handfuls of fresh spinach
- sea salt and fresh ground pepper
- organic rice (brown, basmati or jasmine) OR quinoa, cooked according to package directions

Instructions:

Warm grapeseed oil in large frying pan over low heat for one minute. Turn up heat to medium and add onion, garlic and rosemary. Heat for one more minute, then turn the heat to high and add all of the veggies. Sauté until veggies are slightly tender but still brightly colored. Salt and pepper to taste. Serve over rice or quinoa.

Stuffed Baked Potatoes

by Kelly H, Ypsilanti MI   Serves: 2

INGREDIENTS

    2 large potatoes

    1 Tbsp grapeseed oil (or any healthy oil such as avocado oil or coconut oil)

    1 small onion, sliced

    green, red and yellow peppers, sliced

    optional: mushrooms

    optional: zucchini, sliced

    1 handful of spinach, raw is preferred

    organic cheddar, Monterey Jack or Mexican blend cheese OR vegan cheese

    optional: canned black beans, heated

    organic sour cream OR vegan substitute OR plain Greek yogurt

    guacamole

    Trader Joe's corn salsa

    optional: organic butter

Instructions:

Preheat oven to 350°. Pierce each potato several times with a sharp knife and then place potatoes in baking dish. Bake at least 1 hr or until potato can be easily pierced with a fork.

While the potatoes are baking, prepare veggies and other ingredients. Sauté onion, peppers, mushrooms, zucchini and spinach in oil until tender but still brightly colored.

When potatoes are ready, cut each one length wise and then across, and open it up. Then top with as many of the ingredients as you like.

MAIN DISHES   47

Yellow Squash Stir Fry (eliminate egg for Vegan)
INGREDIENTS

brown rice	broccoli
red pepper	yellow squash
mushrooms	kale
garlic	celery
1 egg	healthy cooking oil

Instructions:
Prepare brown rice separately according to package directions. Combine all other ingredients in a frying pan with a healthy oil (e.g., avocado oil, olive oil or grapeseed oil), then add the egg at the end as you continue to stir. Add cooked brown rice or just top your rice in your bowl or plate with the mixture.

Spicy Stir Fry
INGREDIENTS

grapeseed oil	mushrooms
broccoli	garlic
green onions	yellow pepper
kale	pine nuts
ginger powder	sea salt and cayenne pepper to taste

Stir fry all ingredients in grapeseed oil until veggies are tender but not mushy.

Ginger Garlic Stir Fry

grapeseed oil	onions
garlic cloves	ginger powder
sea salt and pepper	2 kinds of mushrooms
zucchini	yellow squash
celery	red pepper and yellow pepper

Stir fry all ingredients in a healthy oil until veggies are tender but not mushy. Serve on spaghetti squash as an option.

Thai Chicken with Sugar Snap Peas

by Kristi K., Ypsilanti, MI

INGREDIENTS
- ¾ cup Italian dressing, divided
- 1 lb. boneless skinless chicken breasts, cut into thin strips
- 2 Tbsp crunchy peanut butter
- 2 Tbsp honey
- 2 Tbsp light soy sauce
- ½ tsp crushed red pepper
- ½ lb. thin spaghetti, cooked
- 1 pkg (8 oz.) fresh sugar snap peas, rinsed

Instructions:

Pour ¼ cup dressing over chicken in medium bowl; mix lightly. Refrigerate 1 hour to marinate.

Meanwhile, whisk remaining dressing with peanut butter, honey, soy sauce and crushed pepper until blended. Reserve for later use.

Cook spaghetti as directed on package, omitting salt. While spaghetti is cooking, remove chicken from marinade; discard marinade.

Cook and stir chicken in large nonstick skillet on medium heat 5 min. or until chicken is no longer pink. Add peas; cook and stir 3 min. or until chicken is done. Remove skillet from heat.

Drain spaghetti. Add to chicken mixture along with the reserved dressing mixture; mix lightly.

*We make this recipe healthy by using almond butter, coconut aminos instead of soy, our own Italian dressing (so no sugar & added preservatives), and brown rice pasta.

Three Bean Chili

INGREDIENTS

- black, pinto, and kidney beans (we recommend making your beans from dried beans rather than from a can to avoid aluminum)
- organic canned tomatoes
- organic tomato sauce
- garlic powder
- cayenne pepper
- chili powder
- 2 Tbsp quinoa, pre-cooked

Combine all ingredients in a large pot and simmer for 20-30 min.

It's a stir fry kind of day

- grapeseed oil
- garlic
- onion
- celery
- a little bit of kale and a little bit of collard greens
- zucchini
- broccoli
- spices: ginger, turmeric, cumin, onion powder, Mrs. Dash

Stir fry all ingredients in grapeseed oil until veggies are tender but not mushy.
Always experimenting – we will probably have some quinoa with this.

Vegetable Stir Fry

- green beans
- corn (be sure it is organic, non-GMO)
- black beans
- zucchini
- broccoli
- cayenne pepper
- Himalayan salt

Stir fry all ingredients in a healthy oil until veggies are tender but not mushy. Serve over a half of a cooked spaghetti squash.

Curry Stir Fry

by Megan M., Plymouth, MI

INGREDIENTS
- sweet potato chunks
- zucchini
- broccoli
- garlic
- cauliflower
- avocado
- egg
- cayenne pepper
- paprika
- salt
- curry powder

Instructions:

Sauté in grapeseed oil.

Serve on spaghetti squash, quinoa or brown rice.

Broccoli Ginger Stir Fry

Prep Time: 10 mins   Cook Time: 10 mins   Serves: 4

INGREDIENTS
- 2 cups chopped organic broccoli
- 2 cups chopped organic baby carrots
- 1 cup organic peas
- 1 cup organic pea pods
- ½ cup coconut aminos (soy sauce replacement)
- 1-2 Tbsp ginger
- 1 tsp pink salt
- 2 Tbsp coconut oil

Instructions:

Throw all ingredients into a frying pan and cook!

MAIN DISHES   51

Yummy Stir Fry
INGREDIENTS

- snow peas
- broccoli
- purple cabbage
- mushrooms
- celery
- cauliflower
- asparagus
- onions
- carrots
- garlic

Instructions:

Stir fry all ingredients in a healthy oil until veggies are tender but not mushy. Serve over brown rice .

Italian Stir Fry
INGREDIENTS

- mushrooms
- garlic
- half an avocado
- zucchini
- green beans

Sauce:

- ¼ cup grapeseed oil
- cayenne pepper
- Italian seasoning

Instructions:

Serve over spaghetti squash or brown rice

* To make a spaghetti squash, puncture the squash with a sharp knife, place in a baking dish and heat in the oven at 375° for 30 minutes. Remove from oven, cut in half, deseed, then continue baking for 45 - 60 minutes.

Quinoa with Butternut Squash, Cranberries & Pomegranate

Serves: about 4-6

INGREDIENTS

- 1 butternut squash, peeled, seeded, and cubed
- 1 red onion, peeled and diced
- 3-5 cloves garlic, with peel still on
- 1 Tbsp. of any high-heat healthy cooking oil
- salt and pepper
- 1 ½ cups quinoa, rinsed
- 3 cups vegetable broth, or water
- zest of one orange (optional)
- 2 cups roughly-chopped fresh spinach
- 2/3 cup dried cranberries
- ½ cup shelled pistachios (or other nut like walnuts)
- 2/3 cup pomegranate seeds

Directions:

- Preheat oven to 425°. Line a baking sheet with parchment paper.
- In a large mixing bowl, **toss butternut squash**, onion, and garlic cloves (with peel still on) until they are evenly coated with oil. Spread them out in an even layer on the prepared baking sheet. Season generously with salt and pepper. Roast for 30 minutes, or until soft and cooked and the edges begin to slightly brown. Remove and set aside. Discard the garlic peels.
- Meanwhile, stir together quinoa, broth (or water), and orange zest, and cook according to package instructions. When cooked, set aside.
- Add the cooked veggies, quinoa, spinach, cranberries, nuts and seeds to a large mixing bowl, and gently toss to combine. Season with additional salt and pepper if need be. Serve warm or cold.

Avocado Tomato Eggplant Rounds

Prep Time: 5 mins   Cook Time: 20 mins   Total Time: 25 mins

Please use all organic ingredients when possible!

by Megan Lawson   Serves: 2

INGREDIENTS

- 1 small eggplant
- 1 avocado
- 1 tomato, sliced
- ½ tsp garlic powder
- ¼ tsp turmeric
- dash of cayenne pepper
- salt and pepper to taste

Instructions:

Preheat oven to 350°.

Cut eggplant into rounds. Place on baking sheet covered with parchment and bake for 20 minutes. Make sure to keep an eye after 12 minutes. Depending on size and oven heat, they could bake faster. They'll brown a little. You just don't want them to burn.

While they are baking, make the avocado mash using a fork to mix all of the seasonings and avocado together.

When the eggplants are done baking, allow to cool for at least 10 minutes.

Once cool, spread avocado mash, top with tomato and nutritional yeast.

A modified version of a Central American dish

INGREDIENTS

- 1 cup nut butter
- 3 Tbsp of coconut oil or avocado oil
- 1 clove of garlic
- 1 cup of chopped vegetables (you could use carrots, potatoes, peppers, one cup of fresh spinach leaves or any other leafy green vegetable)
- extra water for boiling
- ½ cup of almond milk or purified water
- 1 medium onion

Instructions:

Boil water in a pot. Add the coarsely chopped spinach or greens and boil uncovered for 15 minutes. Strain and discard water, leaving greens in a small bowl. Set aside.

In another small bowl, add the milk or purified water little by little to the nut butter and stir. Set aside.

In the large pot, sauté onion, garlic and vegetables in oil until slightly cooked. Add the nut butter mixture. Mix and simmer on low heat for 2 to 3 minutes. Add the cooked spinach or greens; mix well and simmer for 2 more minutes. Serve with brown rice or a whole grain sprouted tortilla.

Roasted Cabbage

- 1 head cabbage
- 2 Tbsp oil
- 1 tsp salt
- Optional: 1 tsp cumin seeds or caraway seeds

Instructions:

Set oven to 450°F.

Cut cabbage into 8 quarters. Leave the core intact to help hold them together.

Pour the oil on a baking sheet and rub both cut sides of each wedge in the oil. Lay them cut-side-down, and sprinkle with salt and optional spices.

Roast for about 20 minutes, until softened and the outer cabbage leaves are crisp (they are the best part!). Serve hot.

Roasted Cauliflower or Cabbage

Place **1 large cauliflower or cabbage cut into 6 parts** in large baking dish. Surround the cauliflower or cabbage with **diced celery, onion and diced carrots** sprinkled with:

- 1 tsp sage
- 1 tsp rosemary
- 1 tsp thyme
- sea salt & pepper

and sprinkle a bit on top
with the following before baking:

- melted butter
- 4 garlic cloves
- 1 tsp sage
- 1 tsp rosemary
- 1 tsp thyme
- sea salt & pepper

Roast for 1 ½ hrs at 450°.

Gravy:

On stove, heat:

- 3 Tbsp butter
- ½ finely diced onion
- 4 oz diced mushrooms
- 1 tsp sage
- 1 tsp rosemary
- 1 tsp thyme
- garlic (couple of chopped cloves or 1 ½ tsp)
- sea salt & pepper

Cook over heat for around 10 mins.

Add **3 Tbsp garbanzo flour** (or use **corn starch** to thicken). Keep stirring.

Add **2-4 cups veggie broth**. Simmer 10 mins.

Add more flour to thicken if needed.

Food Babe's Spaghetti Squash Casserole

Prep Time: 1 hour   Cook Time: 35 mins   Total Time: 1 hour 35 mins

Serves: 6-8

INGREDIENTS

- 1 large spaghetti squash
- 2 cups vegetable broth
- 1 ½ cups water
- 5 leaves fresh sage minced finely or ½ tsp dried
- 3 cloves garlic, minced
- ¼ tsp turmeric
- fresh ground pepper
- 1 Tbsp fresh lemon juice

- 1 cup dry quinoa
- olive oil for spraying
- ⅛ cup spelt or almond flour
- ½ tsp olive oil
- ¼ tsp sea salt
- ¼ tsp red pepper flakes
- ⅓ cup nutritional yeast
- 1 tsp yellow mustard

Instructions:

Preheat oven to 350°.

Topping:

Make quinoa according to package instructions with vegetable broth instead of water.

Spaghetti Squash:

Slice spaghetti squash in half and remove all seeds with spoon.

Place spaghetti squash face down on large baking sheet, add ½ cup water and cover with foil.

Bake spaghetti squash for 45 mins.

Once baked, take a fork and scrape out inside of squash into a large baking dish.

Cheese Sauce:

Combine water, flour, ground pepper, red pepper flakes, turmeric, and nutritional yeast and mix together to combine. Set aside.

Heat a pan on medium heat, add olive oil and garlic.

Sauté garlic for 2-3 mins, making sure not to burn.

Add sage and cook lightly until fragrant.

Next add the liquid, flour and spice mixture to the pan. The mixture should begin to bubble and start to thicken, if not – increase heat.

Allow sauce to bubble for about 2-3 mins, and then add lemon juice and mustard and cook another 2 mins.

Assembly of Casserole:

Pour cheese sauce evenly over squash in baking dish.

Top with quinoa and lightly spray with olive oil.

Bake at 350° for 20-25 mins and broil on high for last 5-10 mins to brown the top.

Notes:

Makes approximately 6-8 servings. Great as a main dish or side dish for Thanksgiving! Also – this recipe can be made ahead and baked later (for 30-40 mins instead) – A huge time saver! *Cheese Sauce adapted from "Veganomican – The Ultimate Vegan Cookbook".

Lemony Whole Roasted Cauliflower

Serves: 4

INGREDIENTS

1 head cauliflower, outer leaves trimmed

2 Tbsp extra virgin olive oil

zest and juice of 1 lemon

1 Tbsp Dijon mustard

¼ tsp sea salt

¼ cup chopped fresh parsley

Instructions:

Preheat oven to 375°F.

Add whole head of cauliflower (or break into smaller florets) to glass or ceramic baking dish (cauliflower sizes fluctuate, so pick a dish that fits).

In a small bowl, combine oil, lemon zest and juice, mustard and salt. Pour mixture over cauliflower. Then bake 40 minutes to 1 hour until cauliflower is tender when pierced with a knife (time dependent on size of cauliflower). Transfer to serving dish and sprinkle with parsley. Slice into wedges and serve.

Creamy Mushroom Rice/ Quinoa Dish

Prep Time: 10 minutes   Cook Time: 30 minutes   Total Time: 40 minutes

INGREDIENTS
- 1 Tbsp olive oil
- 1 shallot or ½ white onion, diced
- 3 garlic cloves minced
- 1 cup button mushrooms thinly sliced
- 1 cup rice or quinoa
- 2 ¼ cups vegetable stock
- ½ Tbsp white wine vinegar (optional)*
- ¼ cup nutritional yeast flakes (optional)**
- fresh parsley to serve
- salt and pepper to taste

Instructions:
1. Heat the healthy cooking oil in a large sauté pan. Add the shallot and garlic and cook on a medium-low heat until softened.
2. Add the mushrooms and cook for another minute.
3. Stir in the (brown or risotto) rice or quinoa and immediately pour in the stock and vinegar (if using). Bring to a boil, then reduce to a simmer for approximately 30 minutes or until all the liquid has been absorbed and the rice is cooked. Add more hot water, if necessary.
4. Once cooked, stir in the nutritional yeast (if using), stir in a handful of chopped fresh parsley, and season with salt and pepper.
5. Serve and enjoy!

Vegetable and Bean Pot Pies with Potato Crust

Serves: 5

INGREDIENTS

    1 Tbsp extra virgin olive oil, divided
    1 medium yellow onion, small diced
    1 medium carrot, small diced
    1 stalk celery, small diced
    4 cloves garlic, minced
    1 tsp minced fresh rosemary (about 1 sprig)
    1 tsp tomato paste
    1 medium zucchini, cut into ½ inch cubes
    1 ½ cups cooked white beans, like navy or butter beans
    salt and pepper, to taste
    3 Tbsp whole spelt or almond flour
    1 ½ cups vegetable stock
    1 medium sweet potato or 6 to 7 mini new potatoes, thinly sliced, or a mixture

Instructions:

- Preheat oven to 375°. Place 5 ramekins or ovenproof dishes with 1 cup capacity on a baking sheet and set aside.
- Heat half the olive oil in large pot over medium heat. Add onions, carrots and celery, and sauté until onions are slightly softened, about 3 minutes. Add garlic, rosemary and tomato paste, and stir. Add zucchini and white beans to pot. Stir to combine. Season stew with salt and pepper.
- Sprinkle flour over vegetables and beans. Stir until flour is moistened and is starting to get slightly pasty. Pour in vegetable stock. Bring to a boil and then reduce to a simmer until slightly thickened, stirring occasionally, about 4 minutes.
- Divide stew among the 5 ramekins. Arrange sweet potato slices on top of ramekins in a fan or layered pattern. This will form your top crust. Gently brush the sweet potato slices with remaining oil. Season crusts with salt and pepper.
- Slide pot pies into the oven, and bake until the filling is bubbling and the sweet potato slices are tender and lightly browned on the edges, about 30 to 35 minutes.
- Serve pot pies hot.

Gingered Sweet Potato and Mung Bean Curry with Coconut
Serves: 5   Ready in 1 Hour

    1 Tbsp virgin coconut oil
    1 yellow onion, finely chopped
    2 cloves garlic, minced
    2-inch piece of fresh ginger peeled and minced
    1 tsp ground cumin
    ½ tsp crushed red pepper flakes
    ¼ tsp ground cinnamon
    ¼ tsp ground turmeric
    ½ cup mung beans, rinsed
    1 medium sweet potato, peeled and 1 inch diced
    4 cups vegetable stock
    14 oz can light coconut milk
    1 tsp coconut aminos
    3 cups baby spinach, lightly packed
    ½ cup cilantro leaves, roughly chopped
    1 Tbsp fresh lime juice
    sea salt and ground black pepper, to taste

- Heat coconut oil in large, heavy soup pot over medium heat. Add onions and sauté until lightly softened, about 3 minutes. Add garlic, ginger, cumin, red pepper flakes, cinnamon and turmeric to pot. Stir and cook until garlic is quite fragrant, about 30 secs. Add mung beans and sweet potato and stir to coat in the spices and onions. Pour vegetable stock into pot and stir again. Cover and bring stew to a boil. Then, reduce heat to a simmer. Cook stock, covered, until mung beans are just tender, about 25 mins.
- Pour coconut milk and coconut aminos into pot and stir. Bring stew to a boil once more. Add spinach, cilantro, lime juice, salt and pepper, and stir until spinach is wilted and bright green, about 2 mins. Check stew seasoning and adjust if necessary.

Lentil (or other bean) Burritos

INGREDIENTS
- 2 cups cooked lentils (or other beans if you prefer)
- healthy oil (grapeseed, macadamia nut or avocado oil)
- a little onion
- sea salt and pepper
- salsa
- jalapeño, diced
- soft spinach tortillas OR Ezekiel tortillas
- vegan cheese OR high-quality dairy cheese

Instructions:

Fry up the lentils in a pan with grapeseed, macadamia nut, or avocado oil with sea salt and pepper and a little onion. Once they are at a good consistency, add some organic salsa (mild, medium, hot). We also add a jalapeño (diced) to make it spicier.

Purchase soft spinach tortillas (my favorite) or Ezekiel tortillas for the "wrap" and vegan cheese made from cashews with a Mexican flavor or use a high-quality dairy cheese (remember no hormones or antibiotics).

Place a scoop of lentil mixture in the center of the tortilla, pile on some vegan cheese, roll up and place in a baking dish.

Once you have filled all the wraps/tortillas, sprinkle with cheese you have saved for the top, and heat in the oven at 375° until the cheese melts. Enjoy with Beanito chips and salsa.

Peanut Butter Chia Overnight Oats

Serves: 1

INGREDIENTS

- ¾ cup organic rolled oats
- 2 Tbsp chia seeds
- ½ tsp cinnamon
- pinch of sea salt
- 1 cup unsweetened vanilla almond milk (or any plant milk)*
- ½ cup filtered water
- 1 tsp vanilla extract (optional)
- 1 ripe banana, mashed (but leave a few banana coins for topping!)
- 2 Tbsp organic peanut powder + 1 ½ Tbsp water (or any nut butter, to taste if not using powder)
- 1-2 Tbsp maple syrup, raw honey, or a few drops of liquid stevia for extra sweetness

Extras/Toppings:

- cacao nibs (optional)
- crushed almonds or walnuts
- extra sprinkles of cinnamon!
- coconut flakes
- sliced banana coins

Instructions:

Add oats, chia seeds, cinnamon, and sea salt to a mason jar and mix well. Add in almond milk, water, vanilla, and mashed banana. Stir until combined.

In a small bowl, mix peanut powder with water until creamy. You can double the ingredients for extra peanut buttery flavor! Stir "peanut butter" mixture into mason jar. You can add toppings now or in the morning!

Refrigerate overnight or at least 4 hours. Dig in with a spoon and enjoy!

Notes:

* Other plant milk options: coconut milk, hemp milk, rice milk, flax milk, oat milk, cashew milk, etc.

** If overnight oats seem too dry for your liking in the morning, just add in a couple splashes of almond milk or water!

Raw, Vegan Breakfast Pudding

Serves: 6-8

INGREDIENTS

- **4 cups cashew milk**
- **1 banana (ripe works best)**
- **½ cup raw flaked oats (you can use organic rolled oats)**
- **½ cup chia seeds**
- **3 cups fresh fruit (strawberries, blueberries and raspberries)**
- **1 tsp vanilla (optional)**
- **pinch Himalayan sea salt (optional)**

Instructions:

1. Blend banana into cashew milk.
2. Stir in the remaining ingredients.
3. Ladle into jars, cover and place in refrigerator overnight. Alternatively, you can just put in a glass bowl, cover and refrigerate overnight. It will be ready to go in the morning!

Oats are a great source of fiber. They also contain protein, thiamin, magnesium, phosphorus, zinc, manganese, selenium and iron. They are filling and help prevent heart disease! Chia seeds are high in omega 3's. Something that many of us are lacking. They also have fiber, protein, antioxidants and a wonderful filling quality, like the oats. And cashews are one of the healthiest nuts. They protect your heart and your bones, and studies have shown that a moderate amount of nuts can actually help you lower your risk of weight gain. If you don't like cashews, you can always substitute your favorite nut milk.

SOUPS

Interesting Soup

INGREDIENTS

- 1 sweet dumpling squash (or acorn or buttercup squash), baked
- 1 container of vegetable broth
- a little bit of unsweetened coconut milk
- ginger
- sea salt
- cinnamon
- nutmeg

Instructions:

Bake squash whole in oven at 350° for at least an hour (be sure to puncture with a knife before baking); let cool enough to handle. Then scoop out seeds and discard. Then scoop out the squash and combine with the rest of the ingredients in a large pot and simmer 20 to 30 minutes. Adjust spices to taste.

Veggie Soup

INGREDIENTS

- 1 container of veggie broth
- 1 white potato
- 1 sweet potato
- 1 cup cabbage
- kale
- a little parsley
- several carrots
- ½ a medium onion
- a couple stalks of celery
- 2 cloves of garlic
- 1 cup brown rice
- ginger powder
- sea salt, pepper, and turmeric to taste

Instructions:

Combine all ingredients in a large pot and simmer for 20-30 min until veggies are tender. Yum!

Creamy Vegan Corn Chowder

Prep time: 5 mins   Cook time: 25 mins   Total time: 30 mins
A quick, simple and healthy soup made with corn, potatoes, celery and red pepper.
by Crazy Vegan Kitchen   Serves: 4

INGREDIENTS

- 1 Tbsp olive oil
- 1 red pepper, diced
- 1 medium potato, peeled and diced
- 1 cup almond/oat milk
- 1 tsp celery salt
- 1 tsp dried parsley
- 1 tsp apple cider vinegar
- chopped green onion, for garnish
- 1 yellow onion, diced
- 2 sticks of celery, diced
- 3 Tbsp almond flour
- 2 cups vegetable broth
- 1 tsp smoked paprika
- 4 ears of corn, shucked
- salt/pepper, to taste
- cilantro, for garnish
- extra bits of corn and red pepper, for garnish

Instructions:

In a large pot, heat olive oil. Sauté onion, red pepper and celery for 10 minutes or until soft. Add diced potato and mix well. Once mixed, add in flour and stir to coat veggies. Cook for a minute or two before adding your non-dairy milk of choice and vegetable broth.

Add celery salt, smoked paprika and dried parsley into the pot. Stir well and then bring to a boil. Once at a boil, reduce to simmer, cover pan with a lid and simmer gently for 15-20 minutes, or until potato bits are tender.

Once potato is tender, add shucked corn kernels and stir to combine. Let cook for another 5-10 minutes or until corn is tender to your liking.

Transfer ¼ - ⅓ of the soup to a blender (depending on how thick you want the chowder) and blend till smooth. Pour back into the pot and stir well. (Or use an immersion blender.) Stir in apple cider vinegar and taste to adjust seasoning before serving. Top with chopped green onion, cilantro and extra bits of corn/red pepper.

Red Lentil Soup with Lemon

Time: 45 minutes Serves: 4

This is a lentil soup that defies expectations of what lentil soup can be. It is light, spicy and a bold red color (no murky brown here): a revelatory dish that takes less than an hour to make. The cooking is painless.

INGREDIENTS
- 3 Tbsp olive oil, more for drizzling
- 1 large onion, chopped
- 2 garlic cloves, minced
- 1 Tbsp tomato paste
- 1 tsp ground cumin
- ¼ tsp sea salt, more to taste
- ¼ tsp ground black pepper
- pinch of ground chili powder or cayenne, more to taste
- 1 quart chicken or vegetable broth
- 2 cups water
- 1 cup red lentils
- 1 large carrot, peeled and diced
- juice of ½ lemon, more to taste
- 3 Tbsp chopped fresh cilantro

Instructions:

Sauté onion and garlic in oil, then stir in tomato paste, cumin, and chili powder and cook a few minutes more to intensify flavor. Add broth, water, red lentils (which cook faster than their green or black counterparts), and diced carrot, and simmer for 30 minutes. Purée half the mixture and return it to the pot for a soup that strikes the balance between chunky and pleasingly smooth. A hint of lemon juice adds an up note that offsets the deep cumin and chili flavors.

Featured in: "A Lentil Soup To Make You Stop, Taste And Savor"
https://www.nytimes.com/2008/01/09/dining/09appe.html.

Cauliflower Coconut Oil, Ginger and Turmeric Stew

by Ginny B., Fort Myers, FL

INGREDIENTS

- 2 Tbsp organic coconut oil
- 1 tsp cumin seeds
- 1 medium onion finely chopped
- 3 ripe tomatoes
- 1 medium organic cauliflower cut into bite sized pieces
- 1 jalapeño stemmed, seeded and chopped
- 1 cup chopped organic kale
- 2 tsp ginger paste
- 1 Tbsp cumin powder
- 1 Tbsp coriander powder
- 1 can full fat unsweetened coconut milk
- 1 tsp sea salt
- 1 tsp turmeric
- 2 Tbsp fresh chopped cilantro

Instructions:

In a medium stock pot, heat coconut oil for 30 seconds and add cumin seeds and stir until sputter. Add onions and cook another minute. Add tomatoes, stir and cook for a few more minutes until tomatoes are soft. Add the rest of the ingredients and stir and cover. Simmer for about 15 minutes, stirring to keep from burning. Ladle soup into 4 serving bowls and enjoy.

I tripled recipe. Add enough jalapeño peppers to flavor.

Taco Soup

INGREDIENTS
- 1 carton vegetable broth
- 2 cans of black beans
- 2 cans tomatoes
- 1 can or 1 small frozen package of corn
- 1 packet of taco seasoning
- 1 – 1 ½ cups uncooked quinoa
- nutritional yeast

Instructions:

Add all ingredients (except nutritional yeast) in a pot and let simmer for 30 minutes, stirring occasionally. Serve into bowls and sprinkle with nutritional yeast.

Avocado Cashew Soup

Serves: 2

- 1 avocado
- 2 green onions, chopped
- 1 tsp of pink salt
- 1 organic cucumber
- juice of 1 lime
- 1 cup of cashew cream

Instructions:

To make Cashew Cream: 1 cup cashews   1 cup water

Soak 1 cup cashews in cold water for two hours.
Drain cashews and rinse.
Place in blender with 1 cup water.
Blend on high for several minutes until creamy.

To Make Soup:

For the soup, chop cucumber, avocado, and green onions and combine with 1 cup cashew cream in a blender or food processor.

Add lime juice, salt, and pepper and blend until smooth. Garnish with fresh tomatoes, cilantro, or avocado slices.

Chicken & Rice Soup

INGREDIENTS (All organic)

chicken (2 pieces, cooked)	chicken broth
cayenne pepper	curry
poultry seasoning	paprika
brown rice (cooked)	3 long carrots
2 baby sweet peppers	¼ onion (diced)
1 potato	2 garlic cloves

Instructions:

Combine all ingredients in a large pot and simmer for 20-30 min until veggies are tender.

Sweet and Potato Soup

INGREDIENTS

- 1 carton of veggie broth
- 2 cups coconut milk
- filtered water
- ½ diced onion
- 4 carrots
- 3 or 4 sweet potatoes; and 3 or 4 organic white Idaho or organic red potatoes
- sea salt and pepper
- Bragg's organic sprinkle herbs and spices
- cumin to taste
- 2 or 3 drops of Young Living Vitality Basil
- 2 or 3 drops of Young Living Vitality Rosemary

Instructions:

Add all ingredients into a pot and simmer on low heat for 30 minutes. Add additional filtered water to cover all ingredients while simmering. Serve and enjoy.

Lentil Soup

INGREDIENTS
- dried lentils
- onion
- celery
- carrots
- vegetable broth
- sea salt and pepper
- cumin (optional)
- ginger powder (optional)
- fresh spinach

Instructions:

Cook dried lentils as instructed on package. When about ¾ of the way done, add onion, celery, carrots, vegetable broth, and spices: sea salt, pepper, occasionally I add cumin and ginger powder. When finished, add some fresh spinach and simmer until it is a bit wilted. Enjoy!

Chicken and Avocado Soup

by KristyAnn

INGREDIENTS
- 2 tsp olive oil
- 2 cloves garlic, minced
- 5 cups reduced sodium chicken broth
- 2 cups shredded cooked chicken breast (12 oz)
- 8 ounces (2 small) ripe Hass avocados, diced
- 1/3 cup chopped cilantro
- sea salt and fresh pepper, to taste
- pinch chipotle chili powder (optional)
- 1 ½ cups scallions, chopped fine
- 1 medium tomato, diced
- 4 lime wedges
- 1/8 teaspoon cumin

Instructions:

In large pot, sauté scallions and garlic in olive oil until tender. Then add all the remaining ingredients and simmer for 20 – 30 minutes. Enjoy.

Cabbage Soup

INGREDIENTS

- 3 - 15oz cans fire-roasted tomatoes
- 3 - 15oz cans tomato sauce
- 2 cups quinoa (cooked separately)
- 2 packages pre-shredded cabbage
- 2-3 Tbsp Italian seasoning
- 1 Tbsp fresh garlic
- 1 Tbsp cayenne pepper
- water

Instructions:

Mix all ingredients in a crockpot and stir. Add water until it reaches the top of the cabbage. Let it simmer overnight. (Or cook on high in crockpot for 2 hours.)

Notes:

Meat eaters – feel free to add ground beef or turkey that is hormone/antibiotic free instead of the quinoa (a pound fried up and added to all the ingredients).

For extra heat, add jalapeno peppers and/or some organic Sriracha sauce.

Pumpkin Butternut Squash Soup

INGREDIENTS

- 1 butternut squash
- 1 can organic pumpkin
- 2 cups coconut milk
- purified water
- 1 Tbsp minced garlic
- sea salt
- pepper
- 1 tsp turmeric
- 1 tsp ginger
- a pinch of cayenne pepper
- raw organic pumpkin seeds

Instructions:

Bake butternut squash whole in oven at 350° for at least an hour (be sure to puncture with a knife before baking); let cool.

In a large pot, add one can of organic pumpkin, 2 cups coconut milk, purified water, one Tbsp minced garlic, sea salt and pepper, 1 tsp of turmeric, 1 tsp ginger, and a pinch of cayenne pepper.

Add the butternut squash scooping out most of the seeds.

Smash in with the liquid in the pot then simmer on the stove for 20 to 30 minutes Dish out in your bowls to serve and sprinkle with raw organic pumpkin seeds.

Vegan Mushroom Soup

by Brenda M. Livonia, MI

INGREDIENTS

- 2 Tbsp olive oil
- 6 cups sliced portabella mushrooms
- 3 celery stalks chopped in small pieces
- 1 white onion chopped in small piece
- 2 Tbsp minced fresh garlic
- 4 cups vegetable broth
- 4 cups almond milk
- ¾ cup garbanzo bean flour
- thyme to taste
- paprika to taste
- dash of nutmeg
- salt and pepper to taste

Instructions:

Sauté mushrooms, celery, onion and garlic in olive oil for about 5 minutes. Add 3 cups of vegetable broth. With the remaining broth, whisk flour until smooth. Gradually add flour mixture to pan, stirring constantly until thickened. Add almond milk, stirring constantly. Once soup has boiled and base is thickened, add seasonings to taste. I tend to like a lot of paprika and thyme.

Spicy African Yam Soup (Vegan)

INGREDIENTS

- sweet potatoes (2)
- black beans (2 cans)
- Sriracha sauce
- zucchini (2)
- water
- regular potatoes (2)
- hot salsa
- garlic
- brown rice
- vegetable stock

Instructions:

Add all ingredients into a pot and simmer on low heat for 30 minutes.

Mild African Yam Soup

*by Kelly H, Ypsilanti, MI

INGREDIENTS

    1 Tbsp organic grass fed butter, coconut oil or grapeseed oil
    1 small or medium onion, chopped
    1 large sweet potato, peeled and diced
    1 clove garlic, minced
    4 cups organic chicken broth
    1 tsp dried thyme
    ½ tsp ground cumin
    1 cup mild chunky salsa
    1 (15.5 oz.) can garbanzo beans, drained
    1 cup diced zucchini
    ½ cup cooked rice
    sea salt, pepper, apple pie spice to taste
    2 Tbsp creamy organic peanut butter or almond butter

Instructions:

1. Heat oil/butter in a large pot over medium heat. Sauté the onions, sweet potato and garlic until onion is soft. Turn down heat, if necessary, to prevent burning.
2. Stir in the chicken broth, thyme and cumin. Bring to a boil, cover and simmer for about 15 min.
3. Stir in salsa, garbanzo beans and zucchini. Simmer until tender (about 15 min).
4. Stir in the cooked rice and peanut/almond butter until the nut butter has dissolved.

*original recipe from WellnessMama.com

"Creamy" Zucchini, Walnut and Thyme Soup

The "creamy" part comes from souped and blended walnuts. Use good quality nuts—they are important for taste as well as texture. I have written this up with walnuts and thyme, but I just know it would be fabulous with mint, basil and pine nuts.

Serves: 4

INGREDIENTS

    1 cup skin-on walnuts – toast for five minutes at 350°F
    1 large onion, chopped
    1 ½ Tbsp olive oil
    1 ½ tsp dried thyme leaves (less if yours are quite strong-tasting)
    2 bay leaves
    4 garlic cloves, minced
    6 cups chopped zucchini/summer squash – yellow or green
    5 cups vegetable broth
    zest of half a lemon (more to taste)
    freshly ground pepper
    fresh thyme leaves (lemon thyme if you have some) OR ground thyme spice (or you can try thyme essential oil)

Instructions:

1. Heat the oil in a soup pot and add the onions. Sauté gently until translucent. Add the bay leaves, dried thyme and garlic, and sauté a few more minutes. When the garlic smells fragrant and the onions lose their raw smell, add the chopped zucchini and the walnuts. Stir and pour over the hot stock. Bring to a boil. Lower the heat to simmer and cook gently for 20 minutes, adding the lemon zest during the last minute or so.

2. Remove the pan from the heat and fish out the bay leaves. Ladle into a blender or use a hand-blender/immersion blender to blend the soup to a beautifully smooth texture. Test for seasoning and taste – adding pepper, salt and/or honey if need be. Add in the fresh thyme leaves, if using.

Apple Salsa Multigrain Soup

by Kelly H, Ypsilanti, MI

INGREDIENTS

- 1 Tbsp organic grass fed butter
- ½ medium onion, diced
- several mushrooms (broken into pieces, if preferred)
- 1 small apple (I used Pink Lady variety), diced
- ¼ - ½ cup uncooked quinoa
- ¼ cup Trader Joe's Super Seed & Ancient Grain blend OR
    - ¼ cup blend of any of these: chia seeds, flax seeds, hemp seeds, amaranth, sprouted buckwheat, sprouted millet
- 1 carton vegetable broth
- ¼ - ½ cup salsa (whatever spice level you like)
- sea salt, pepper, apple pie spice to taste
- 1 - 2 large handfuls fresh spinach

Instructions:

In a large pot, melt butter and sauté the onions and mushrooms over low heat. Once they begin to soften, add in the diced apple. Allow to soften briefly, and then add the rest of the ingredients except for the spinach. Cover and simmer over low heat for 20 to 30 minutes. Stir in the spinach, cover, and simmer for a few minutes longer until the spinach is wilted. Serve and enjoy.

SIDE DISHES

Sweet Potato Casserole

INGREDIENTS

- 1 ½ lbs sweet potatoes, peeled and cut into 1 inch cubes
- 1 Tbsp + 1 tsp organic grass-fed butter
- 1 Tbsp + 1 tsp raw honey
- ½ tsp sea salt
- ¼ tsp ground cinnamon
- 1 dash ground nutmeg
- ¼ tsp freshly grated ginger (or 1 dash ground ginger)
- ½ cup chopped raw pecans

Instructions:

1. Preheat oven to 375 F.

2. Place sweet potatoes in a large mixing bowl; set aside.

3. Place butter, honey, salt, cinnamon, nutmeg, and ginger in small saucepan; cook over medium heat, stirring occasionally, for 1 - 2 minutes, or until butter is completely melted and ingredients are thoroughly combined.

Curry Quinoa

INGREDIENTS

    1 cup raw quinoa (to be cooked)   1 cup or more raw spinach
    1 tsp cumin   salt/pepper
    2-3 tsp curry
    1 cup beans of your choice (e.g., lentils, black beans, cannelloni)

Instructions:

Prepare quinoa according to package directions. About 10 minutes before quinoa is finished, add at least a cup of raw spinach or more according to your liking.

Keep stirring and once the spinach is slightly wilted, add spices: salt, pepper, cumin. Then add 2-3 tsp of curry depending on the flavor you are going after.

Add 1 can of beans of your choice. Add the entire can including the liquid and stir until heated. Enjoy!

Garlic Mushrooms

INGREDIENTS

    grapeseed oil
    1 pound mushrooms, trimmed, halved or quartered
    3 cloves garlic, peeled and crushed
    salt and freshly ground black pepper

Instructions:

Preheat oven to 450°. Lightly oil shallow baking pan large enough to hold mushrooms in single layer. Add mushrooms and toss with 2 - 3 Tbsp oil. Add garlic; season with salt; roast for 20 minutes, stirring on occasion; mushrooms should be browned. Season with pepper.

Quinoa Side Dish

INGREDIENTS

- quinoa
- garlic powder or several cloves
- kale
- onion
- sea salt and pepper
- grapeseed oil or other healthy oil
- sweet potatoes, cubed
- mushrooms, sliced or diced
- cabbage

Instructions:

Sauté in oil: quinoa, garlic powder or cloves, sweet potatoes (cook briefly before cutting, it will make it easier), and kale. Add mushrooms, onion, cabbage, sea salt and pepper. Enjoy.

Note: you can buy frozen packages of organic kale and quinoa seasoned with garlic, olive oil and salt at Costco.

Sweet Potato Fries

INGREDIENTS

- 1 or 2 sweet potatoes
- ¼ cup grapeseed oil
- cinnamon
- sea salt
- cayenne pepper (optional)

Instructions:

Peel the sweet potatoes, and cut into wedges.

Put potatoes into a bowl, and mix with ¼ cup grapeseed oil, cinnamon and sea salt OR a combination of cayenne pepper and sea salt.

Place on cooking tray.

Sprinkle with more cinnamon or cayenne.

Bake at 350° for 45-60 minutes.

Sweet Potato Skins

Prep Time: 10 mins   Cook Time: 35 mins   Total Time: 45 mins

Serves: 8

INGREDIENTS

    8 small sweet potatoes
    coconut oil
    3 avocados, peeled and pitted
    1 large tomato, diced
    ½ cup diced red onion
    ½ jalapeño, diced
    1 lime, juiced
    ¼ cup chopped cilantro
    sea salt and pepper, to taste
    1 cup cooked black beans
    1 cup shredded vegan cheddar cheese

Instructions:

- Preheat oven to 400°.
- Rub each sweet potato with coconut oil and place in the oven for 25-30 minutes or until fork tender.
- While the sweet potatoes are cooking, in a bowl, make the **guacamole**. Start by mashing the avocado and then add the tomato, onion, jalapeño, lime juice, and cilantro. Season with salt and pepper to taste. Set aside.
- When the sweet potatoes are done, take them out of the oven. Cut each one in half and scoop out half of the filling. Set the filling aside.
- Sprinkle some of the black beans and cheese on each sweet potato half and place back in the oven to melt the cheese, 3-4 minutes.
- When melted, take out of the oven and top with a scoop of guacamole. Enjoy!

Notes:
Please use all organic ingredients if possible Use leftover sweet potato filling as a side dish or freeze for later.

SIDE DISHES

Loaded Sweet Potatoes

So easy & yummy!

INGREDIENTS

- **peppers**
- **onions**
- **tomatoes**
- **black beans**
- **fresh or frozen spinach**
- **avocado**
- **sweet potatoes**

Instructions:

Bake sweet potatoes at 350° for 45-60 min. Remove from oven and cut in half.

Sauté peppers, onions, tomatoes, black beans, spinach, and avocado, and top the sweet potato with this mixture. If you want, you can add **shredded chicken** or **ground turkey**.

Kale Pesto

INGREDIENTS

- **2 cups kale, packed, roughly chopped, stems removed**
- **2 cloves garlic or more to taste**
- **zest of 1 lemon**
- **juice of 1 ½ lemons or more to taste**
- **¼ cup raw almonds**
- **½ cup extra virgin olive oil**
- **¼ tsp sea salt or to taste**
- **¼ tsp pepper or to taste**

Instructions:

Place all ingredients in food processor on Low to reach desired texture.

*Serve Kale Pesto over zoodles – (zucchini noodles)

White Bean Dip with Dill, Lemon and Garlic

Serves: 6-8

INGREDIENTS

    3 cups cooked white beans (from 1 cup dried beans)
    3 Tbsp freshly squeezed lemon juice
    3 Tbsp + 1 tsp extra virgin olive oil
    2 Tbsp chopped dill
    2 garlic cloves, crushed
    finely grated zest of 1 lemon
    1 ¼ tsp coarse sea salt
    ground black pepper
    paprika for garnish

Instructions:

To prepare the dip, puree the beans in a food mill or mash by hand in a medium bowl. Add the lemon juice, 3 Tbsp of oil, dill, garlic cloves lemon zest, 1 ¼ tsp salt, and pepper to taste. Transfer to a serving bowl and refrigerate until you are ready to serve.

Just before serving, season with additional salt to taste, dust with paprika and drizzle with remaining 1 tsp of oil.

Balsamic Drizzled Brussels Sprouts

Serves: 6-8

If you're looking for an appetizing way to prepare Brussels sprouts, look no further than this Balsamic Drizzled Brussels Sprouts recipe from *Naturally Savvy*. The balsamic vinegar adds that much needed flavor to the Brussels sprouts, and in no time your family and friends might be back for seconds.

INGREDIENTS

- 2 pounds Brussels sprouts, trimmed and halved
- 2 Tbsp coconut oil
- 2 cloves garlic, finely chopped
- large pinch of Himalayan salt
- freshly ground black pepper
- 1-2 Tbsp balsamic vinegar (add more or less to taste)

Instructions:

Heat oven to 400°F.

On a large rimmed baking sheet or in a large casserole dish, toss the Brussels sprouts with oil, garlic, salt and a few grinds of freshly ground pepper.

Roast until tender and slightly golden, approximately 25 minutes.

For a crispier texture, switch to broil and leave in oven about 5 more minutes.

Remove from the oven and drizzle with 1-2 Tbsp (or more) of balsamic vinegar.

Taste and adjust seasoning if necessary.

Roasted Brussel Sprouts

INGREDIENTS

- 1 ½ pounds Brussels sprouts, ends trimmed and yellow leaves removed
- 1 tsp sea salt
- ½ tsp freshly ground black pepper
- 3 Tbsp coconut oil, or melted ghee

Instructions:

Preheat oven to 400°F.

In a large resealable plastic bag, place all of the ingredients inside and seal the bag, then shake well to coat the Brussels sprouts.

Pour the contents out onto a baking sheet and insert them into the oven.

Bake for 30 minutes, while shaking the pan every 5-7 minutes (this is for browning). If they start to burn, reduce the heat. The Brussels sprouts will come out dark brown, almost black, when they are fully cooked. Serve as soon as you pull them out of the oven. You can add more pepper or salt if needed for seasoning...or really spice them up like I have with some cayenne pepper and other spices!!

Baked, Stuffed Acorn Squash

INGREDIENTS

- 1 acorn squash
- extra virgin olive oil to taste
- thyme to taste
- brown rice, cooked according to package
- ¼ cup chopped walnuts

Instructions:

Preheat oven to 350°.

Puncture squash with a sharp knife. Bake squash for 45 min or until outside is tender.

Remove from oven and carefully cut the squash in half. Scoop out the seeds and discard.

Then add a little bit of olive oil and thyme.

Top with a serving of brown rice and ¼ cup of walnuts.

Thanksgiving Cauliflower

If there's gravy involved, no one's gonna miss the potatoes.

Total Time: 1:45   Cook: 1:30   Serves: 6

INGREDIENTS

- 1 big head of cauliflower
- 4 garlic cloves (skin-on)
- 4 sprigs fresh thyme
- sea salt
- 4 Tbsp butter, melted (divided)
- 6 sage leaves
- 4 sprigs fresh rosemary
- freshly ground black pepper

GRAVY INGREDIENTS

- 1 Tbsp butter
- ½ onion, finely chopped
- 4 oz. cremini mushrooms, finely chopped
- 3 Tbsp unsalted butter
- 3 Tbsp almond flour
- 2-4 cups vegetable stock

Instructions:

- Preheat oven to 450°F.
- Rub the cauliflower all over with melted butter. Season with salt and pepper. Place in cast iron skillet, surrounded by garlic, 4 sage leaves, 2 sprigs of thyme and 2 sprigs of rosemary. Bake for 1 ½ hours until charred in parts and tender throughout, brushing with more melted butter through. Pierce the cauliflower with a paring knife skewer to check the tenderness.
- Make gravy. Chop remaining thyme and rosemary leaves. Melt remaining butter in a small saucepan over medium heat. Add the onion and sauté until beginning to soften, about 3-5 minutes. Stir in the mushrooms and season mixture with salt and pepper. Add herbs and cook until the mushrooms are tender and browned. Add 1-2 cloves of the roasted garlic (skins removed), breaking up the cloves with a whisk or wooden spoon. Stir in flour and cook for 1 minute. Whisk in 2 cups of vegetable stock and bring mixture to a boil. Reduce heat slightly and simmer for 5 minutes, until the mixture has thickened to your desired consistency. Add more vegetable stock if desired.

DESSERTS

Homemade Chocolate Coconut Bars

INGREDIENTS

- 3 Tbsp coconut oil
- ½ cup cocoa OR cacao powder
- 2 Tbsp chia seeds
- ½ tsp concentrated natural vanilla extract
- 3 Tbsp raw honey
- pinch of sea salt
- 1 cup or more coconut flakes
- opt: almonds

Instructions:

Place all ingredients except for the coconut into a medium sized bowl and mix until well combined and looking deliciously chocolatey. Stir in the coconut. Pour the mixture into a glass container, or plastic if you must (maybe line it with parchment paper). Optional: place some individual almonds on top. Place in the fridge to set—or even the freezer with a lid on it. Slice and serve.

It only takes a couple of hours to set. However, the longer you leave it the firmer it will become. I like it best the day after making. Store in the fridge as it will melt at room temperature.

Enjoy knowing you aren't feeding the kids or yourself nasty refined sugars.

Chocolate Fondue

INGREDIENTS

- coconut oil
- almond milk
- cacao powder
- almond butter

Instructions:

Blend all ingredients together. Then dip pieces of **yellow honeydew** into mixture!

Roasted Pear Crumble with Honey Yogurt

Original recipe from usapears.org.

Serves: 4

INGREDIENTS

    ¼ cup rolled oats

    ¼ cup raw almonds, chopped

    2 Tbsp almond flour

    ½ tsp ground cinnamon

    pinch of sea salt

    3 Tbsp honey, divided

    2 Tbsp + 1 tsp extra virgin olive oil divided

    2 firm but ripe Anjou pears or Bartlett pears, halved and cored (can also be made with apples rather than pears)

    2/3 cup coconut milk yogurt (or skip the yogurt altogether)

Instructions:

- Position a rack in the middle of the oven; preheat oven to 375°.
- In a medium bowl, combine the oat, almonds, flour, cinnamon and salt. Drizzle in 2 Tbsp honey and 2 Tbsp olive oil. Stir until mixture looks wet and clumpy.
- Place each pear, cut side up, in an 8 x 8 x 2-inch baking dish. Coat pears with remaining 1 tsp olive oil. Top each pear with some of the crumble mixture.
- Bake until the pears are tender when pierced with a fork and the topping is brown and crisp, 30-35 minutes.
- In a small bowl, stir the remaining 1 Tbsp honey into the yogurt. Spoon the yogurt into 4 shallow bowls, and place the warm pears on top.

Protein Bars

INGREDIENTS

- 2 cups almonds
- ½ cup seeds, ground (flax, chia, pumpkin, or sunflower)
- ½ cup dried prunes, dates or raisins
- ½ cup shredded coconut
- ½ cup almond butter (I've made my own, so easy)
- ½ tsp sea salt
- ½ cup coconut oil, melted
- 1 Tbsp maple syrup or honey (I've made it with both; I prefer maple syrup)
- 2-3 tsp vanilla

Instructions:

Pulse in food processor all ingredients up to the coconut oil.

Melt coconut oil on low heat. Stir in sweetener and vanilla.

Add oil to food processor until paste.

Press into 8X8 glass baking dish.

Chill for 1 hour in fridge.

Healthy No-Bake Nut Butter Oatmeal Cookies

INGREDIENTS

- ½ cup honey
- ¼ cup coconut milk
- ¼ cup coconut oil
- ½ tsp vanilla
- 1 ½ cups quick oats
- ¼ cup organic almond (or peanut) butter or peanut powder (this is what I use)
- 2 Tbsp chia seeds

Instructions:

Combine first four ingredients in saucepan. Bring to a boil and cook 3 minutes. Remove from heat and stir in almond butter, or peanut powder, chia seeds and then quick oats. Drop by teaspoonfuls onto parchment paper or glass plate. Let cool (refrigerate).

Spiced Pumpkin Freezer Fudge

Total time: 2 hrs 10 mins   Cook Time: 2 hrs   Prep Time: 10 mins
by Megan Olson   Serves: 18 bars

This no-bake pumpkin fudge is made with only six wholesome ingredients and absolutely no processed sugar.

TOOLS
- 10x5 baking pan
- parchment paper
- mixing bowl
- spatula

INGREDIENTS
- ½ cup coconut butter
- ¼ cup maple syrup
- ½ tsp vanilla extract
- ¾ cup organic pumpkin purée
- 2 Tbsp coconut flour
- 2 tsp pumpkin spice

Instructions:

Line a baking sheet with parchment paper. Set aside.

In a mixing bowl, mix together the coconut butter, maple syrup and vanilla until smooth.

Add the remaining ingredients and mix until combined. Do not over mix. If the batter is too stiff, add ¼ cup coconut oil and stir until smooth.

Transfer the batter to the prepared baking sheet and spread into a smooth layer.

Place in the freezer for 2 hours or until frozen.

Slice into 18 bars and serve. Keep the leftover bars in the freezer.

DESSERTS   91

Chocolate and Peanut Butter No-bake Cookies

INGREDIENTS

Use all organic...

- **1 1/3 cups of creamy peanut or almond butter**
- **2 tsp of vanilla extract**
- **2 Tbsp of unsweetened cocoa powder**
- **2 cups of unsweetened coconut flakes**
- **2 Tbsp of melted butter**

Instructions:

- Step 1: Prepare a large baking sheet with parchment paper or use a non-stick silicone baking mat.
- Step 2: In a large mixing bowl, combine the peanut butter, vanilla extract, melted butter, coconut flakes, and cocoa powder and stir until well combined (if you like your cookies a little sweeter, feel free to add 1-2 tsp of Stevia).
- Step 3: Scoop the batter onto your prepared baking sheet. Use the back of the spoon to gently shape each scoop into a 3" cookie.
- Step 4: Place in the freezer for 30 minutes to set.
- Step 5: Store in an airtight container in the freezer.

Now you'll be able to satisfy your sweet tooth without feeling guilty about it!

Chocolate Covered Chickpeas

Purchase **dried sea salt chickpeas** in a bag

On stove, stir together to melt:

- **1 cup coconut oil**
- **½ cup or more of cocoa powder**
- **4 packets or several drops of liquid stevia**
- **½ tsp vanilla**
- **2 Tbsp chia seeds (helps bind)**

After melted, add **1 Tbsp of honey** for added sweet and benefits.

Cover the chickpeas in the chocolate mixture, pour into a pan lined with parchment paper and refrigerate until set. Enjoy!

Store them in the refrigerator or freezer.

Guilt Free Apple/ Pear Delight

INGREDIENTS

- **2 Granny Smith apples**
- **2 pears**
- **2 Tbsp coconut oil**
- **2 packets stevia**
- **2 tsp cinnamon + a little more**
- **2 tsp allspice**
- **raisins (optional)**

Instructions:

Place sliced fruit in 2 Tbsp of coconut oil and heat on the stove. Add 2 packets of stevia, 2 tsp cinnamon, 2 tsp allspice, cook until slightly soft. Pour into serving dish, sprinkle with a little more cinnamon. Add raisins or any other accent items you may like. Yum. Enjoy!

Nudge (not fudge)

INGREDIENTS

- **6 Tbsp organic nut butter***
- **3 Tbsp coconut oil**
- **3 Tbsp raw honey**
- **2 Tbsp cocoa or cacao powder**
- **½ tsp concentrated natural vanilla extract**
- **pinch of sea salt**
- **½ cup walnuts or cashews crushed (I placed them in a Ziplock bag and crushed them)**

Instructions:

- Place all ingredients except for the cashews/walnuts into a medium sized bowl and mix until well combined and looking deliciously chocolatey.
- Stir in the nuts.
- Pour the mixture into a silicone loaf tin, or glass container, or plastic if you must.
- Place in the fridge to set – or even the freezer with a lid on it. Slice and serve. It only takes a couple of hours to set. However, the longer you leave it the firmer it will become. I like it best the day after making.
- Store in the fridge as it will melt at room temperature.

Enjoy knowing you aren't feeding the kids or yourself nasty refined sugars.

*You can use organic peanut butter or almond butter or any nut butter or… if you prefer, use organic peanut butter powder like I did. STAY AWAY FROM PB2 – To use the organic powdered peanuts, you will need to add water to create your butter and then measure it out for the recipe.

Chocolate Orange Chia Seed Pudding

CAUTION: You will want to eat more than 1 serving…I did and so did Mike!!!

Total Time: 2 minutes   Serves: 8

INGREDIENTS

- 1 ½ cups almond milk (or other non-dairy milk)
- ⅓ cup (2 oz.) chia seeds
- 5 drops Young Living orange essential oil
- ½ tsp cinnamon
- ½ tsp vanilla
- 3 Tbsp raw cacao powder
- ~5 pitted dates soaked in hot water, then drained

Instructions:

Place all ingredients into blender, like a Vitamix.

Assemble pudding as desired. I just put it in a container and refrigerate for a couple of hours.

Notes/Nutritional Benefits:

- Nothing refined, made with whole food sweetener – dates: Dates are a great source of potassium, fiber, and a source of magnesium, making them great for heart health. The added fiber helps to lessen blood sugar spikes and moderate blood sugar.
- Great source of fiber, 8.5 g, important for blood sugar regulation, satiety, reducing blood pressure, and boosting digestive health.
- High in plant-based calcium, 27% DV, shown to be better absorbed by the body than animal source, it's important for bone and dental health.
- Good source of plant-based iron, 10% DV, important for oxygenation of blood.
- Good source of plant-based protein, 4.3 g, important for tissue repair.

Protein Packed Cookies – by Dr. Jockers

- ½ cup sunflower seeds
- ½ cup high-quality protein powder
- ¼ cup honey
- 1 tsp vanilla
- 1 tsp cinnamon
- 2 Tbsp coconut oil
- 1/8 cup water

Instructions:

Preheat oven to 300°F.

Roughly chop sunflower seeds (or other nuts you may wish to use) in the blender until broken up into chunks.

Place all ingredients into a bowl and stir together. If you notice that it is too crumbly, then try adding in another tablespoon of coconut oil and possibly more water.

Scoop cookies onto a cookie tray.

Gently press the cookies down to flatten.

Makes about 18 cookies.

Bake for about 15 minutes.

> Additional Notes:
>
> You can use 2 cups coconut shreds if you do not have/want sunflower seeds.
>
> You can use any other kind of nut or seed.
>
> You can use any flavored or unflavored protein powder to change up the flavor.
>
> You can put the coconut whipped cream recipe (https://drjockers.com/coconut-whipped-cream/) in between to make an incredible coconut cookie sandwich!

Dr. Jockers Comments:

This is a fun and tasty recipe that is full of fiber, healthy fats and clean protein. It is low carb, ketogenic and helps us to stabilize our blood sugar and burn fat.

If you are following an autoimmune nutrition plan, then you may want to avoid the sunflower seeds and instead use extra coconut flakes. Coconut flakes are a great source of medium chain fats that help us to burn fat and provide immediate fuel for our body and brain. They also provide good fiber for our microbiome.

Stevia is my preferred sweetener because it is one hundred times sweeter than sugar and has no effect on our blood sugar.

You can use a wide variety of protein powders, such as grass-fed whey protein that is full of branched chain amino acids to help support the development of lean body mass.

Incredible Apple Carrot Quinoa Balls

INGREDIENTS
- 1 cup (loosely packed) coarsely grated carrots (about 2 medium)
- ½ cup (packed) coarsely grated peeled apple (about 1 Gala or Fuji works well)
- ½ cup quinoa flakes
- ⅓ cup creamy unsweetened sunflower seed butter (I used organic Sunbutter)
- 3-4 Tbsp pure maple syrup
- 1 Tbsp ground chia seeds
- 1 tsp ground cinnamon
- ¼ tsp baking soda
- ¼ tsp Celtic sea salt or Himalayan salt
- ¼ cup raisins or dried currants

Instructions:

Preheat oven to 350°F, and line a baking sheet with parchment paper.

Grate the carrot in your food processor, and hand grate the apple for the best results.

In a large bowl, combine the carrot and apple with the dry ingredients, and then mix in the sunflower seed butter and maple syrup.

Stir to combine thoroughly and form a cohesive mass of dough. Then mix in the raisins.

Using moist hands, roll tablespoons of the dough into balls and place them 1-2 inches apart on the lined baking sheet.

Bake the balls for about 20 minutes.

Cool completely, and store in an airtight container in the fridge.

Makes about 18 moist and chewy balls.

published by Pure Living Press - Hallie Klecker at Daily Bites.

Healthy Four-Ingredient Breakfast Brownies

Protein packed brownies which are perfectly acceptable for breakfast and need just four ingredients! Moist, soft and gooey on the inside yet tender on the outside, these flourless breakfast brownies are vegan, gluten free, paleo and refined-sugar free!

INGREDIENTS
- 3 medium, overripe bananas
    - OR 1 cup mashed sweet potato
    - OR 1 cup mashed pumpkin
    - OR mix of all 3
- ½ cup smooth nut butter or almond butter (can sub for any nut/seed butter)
- 2 Tbsp to ¼ cup cocoa or cacao powder (more = richer taste)
- 1-2 scoops of protein powder
- handful of chocolate chips, optional (cocoa or cacao nibs or carob)

Instructions:

Preheat oven to 350°. Grease a small cake pan or loaf pan with coconut oil and set aside.

In a small pan on stovetop, melt your nut butter.

In a blender, food processor, or using your hands, combine the mashed mixture, cocoa or cacao powder, protein powder and nut butter until smooth.

Pour the mixture into the greased pan, top with optional chocolate chips and bake for around 20 minutes or until baked through. Remove from the oven and allow to cool completely before slicing into pieces.

> Notes:
> You don't need to blend or process all ingredients, but doing so lends a smoother texture – although I do like my banana chunks in them.
> These brownies are not super sweet, it depends on the protein powder you choose and how sweet it is. Adjust accordingly if you'd like a very sweet brownie by adding a little stevia or honey perhaps.
> Brownies are best kept and enjoyed refrigerated. They are also freezer friendly.
> My (Lillian's) edited version from Arman @ thebigmansworld

Raw Vegan "Cheesecake"

For the Filling:
- 1 ½ cups of raw cashews
- 1 juiced, large lemon (about ¼ cup of juice)
   - or use 2-3 drops of Young Living Lemon Vitality Essential Oil
- 1/3 cup melted coconut oil
- ½ cup plus 2 Tbsp full, fat coconut milk
- ½ cup maple syrup or raw honey (like it sweeter? add a packet or 2 of powdered stevia)

Preparation: Soak the raw cashews for 4-6 hours, or boil water to pour over the cashews and let it soak for an hour before draining.

For the Crust:
- 1 cup of pitted dates, soaked in water
- 1 cup of raw walnuts, almonds, or macadamia nuts (Feel free to mix two or three of these options!)

Preparation: Soak the pitted dates in warm water for 10 minutes, then drain before use.

Instructions:

The Crust:
1. Add the pre-soaked dates into the food processor or blender and process until the dates are broken up into small pieces and form a ball. Remove from the food processor or blender and set to the side.
2. Add nuts and process into a meal. Then add the processed dates until a loose dough forms. You want this crust to stick together when you squeeze it between your fingers. To strike the right balance, add more nuts if too wet, or if it's too dry, add more dates (or a little of the filtered water you soaked the dates in) as it processes.
3. Grease (coconut oil) a 12-count muffin tin and line with slips of parchment paper. The paper will help pop the cheesecakes out when done. Or simply press the crust into a glass pie dish or cake dish. If you double the recipe you could use a parchment lined tin rectangular baking dish.
4. In each tin, scoop 1 Tbsp of the crust and pack it down into the pan. You can use

the bottom of a glass or the back of the spoon to really get inside the muffin cups. If the crust is sticking too much to the glass, you can use parchment paper to help keep them separated. Let the pan sit in the freezer to firm up the crust.

The Filling:
1. Add your cashews, coconut oil, lemon juice, coconut oil, maple syrup, and coconut milk (the dense, creamier part will make the cheesecake extra creamy, but don't worry if it's all mixed in with the rest of the milk) into a blender. Then blend into a smooth mixture. Try messing with your puree and liquefy settings to help get the mixture to a smooth finish, adding a little bit of coconut milk, lemon juice, or syrup to help it get there.
2. If you are going to use a nut butter: simply blend it into the filling. If you decide to add a fruit, you will swirl it on top as you set the filling inside the cups or just spoon it on top as you serve the cakes individually.
3. Divide up the blended mixture into the cups as evenly as possible, and add your fruit toppings as you go. Once all filled, tap the tins to release any air bubbles, cover in plastic wrap, and freeze for 4-6 hours.
4. Once set, you can remove them from the pan using a butter knife or pulling on the parchment paper. Serve it up frozen, or let it soften for about 10 minutes!
5. And that's it! The basic filling is so good, you'll want to try it with as many topping combinations as possible. It's a great dessert to introduce to a cooked food eater who might be skeptical about raw food. Try it out!

For the Toppings:
You pick one (or more!)

¼ cup blueberries   ¼ cup strawberries, halved
¼ cup raspberries   ¼ cup pitted cherries
2 Tbsp of your favorite nut butter (peanut, almond, hazelnut)

You have so many options to choose from besides the one we mentioned above when it comes to picking a cheesecake flavor! You can even decide to make a sauce for the top, or add a crumble of your favorite raw chocolate. Get creative!

If you decide to use a nut butter, it will get added into the cheesecake as it sets. For fruit, we like to add it on top of the plain cheesecake recipe.

Raw Lemon Cranberry Cheesecake

by Tess Masters - the blender girl

INGREDIENTS

Crust:
- 1 cup whole raw almonds
- 1 cup firmly packed chopped pitted dates plus more as needed

Filling:
- 3 cups raw unsalted cashews, soaked
- 1 ½ cups fresh cranberries
- ¾ cup melted virgin coconut oil
- ¾ cup pure maple syrup
- ½ cup unsweetened almond milk
- 1 Tbsp lemon zest
- ½ cup fresh lemon juice
- 1 tsp natural vanilla extract
- pinch sea salt

Instructions:

1. To make the crust, place the almonds and dates into a food processor fitted with the s blade until well combined and formed into a ball. (You may need to add a few more dates.)
2. Grease a 9-inch springform cake tin with coconut oil, and press the crust into the bottom of the pan. Set aside.
3. To make the filling, place all of the filling ingredients into the blender, and blast on high for about 1 minute until smooth and creamy.
4. Pour the filling into the tin, and gently wiggle so that the cake is even.
5. Cover this tin with aluminum foil, and place in the freezer for 6 to 8 hours. Then transfer to the fridge, and leave it there until you're ready to serve.
6. To serve, gently remove cake from the tin, cut into slices, and serve with raw cashew cream and lemon zest.
7. *Note: This cake will melt if left out at room temperature due to the coconut oil.

DESSERTS

No Bake Cookies

INGREDIENTS

½ cup raw honey
¼ cup coconut milk (or almond milk)
½ tsp vanilla
¼ cup almond butter (or cashew, sunflower, organic peanut butter)
2 Tbsp cocoa or cacao (reg. or dark)
¼ cup coconut oil
1 ½ - 1 ¾ cup quick oats

Instructions:

Combine first five ingredients in saucepan. Bring to boil and cook 2 ½-3 min. Turn off heat and stir in almond butter till smooth, then add quick oats and stir till coated. Drop by teaspoonfuls onto parchment paper. Let cool. It may help the firmness to refrigerate them for at least 30 min.

**Add some unsweetened coconut with the oats for variety, and some chia seeds for binding a bit better OR add more nut butter and limit the cocoa or cacao and they will taste more like peanut butter cookies.

No-Bake Cacao Goji Berries Bars

INGREDIENTS

2 cups coconut oil
2 cups cacao powder
4 Tbsp raw honey (add some stevia if you want it sweeter)
1 cup dried goji berries
1-1½ cups crushed walnuts, almonds, cashews, pumpkin seeds
½ cup chia seeds
1 cup coconut flakes

Instructions:

Melt coconut oil on stove over low heat, add cacao powder and mix well. Add honey and stir for a few minutes. Turn off heat and add remaining ingredients. Pour into a parchment paper lined pan and refrigerate for at least 90 minutes. Feel free to sprinkle additional **coconut flakes** or **nuts** on top before refrigerating.

Sweet Potato Brownies (MY VERSION)

INGREDIENTS
- 1 cup mashed sweet potato
- ½ cup smooth nut butter of choice (I recommend almond or cashew butter – or the organic peanut powder from Costco – add water)
- 2 Tbsp maple syrup or raw honey
- ¼ cup cocoa or cacao powder
- handful of carob chips (optional)

Instructions:
Preheat oven to 350°F and grease a small cake/loaf pan.
On the stove, melt nut butter with maple syrup/honey.
In a large bowl add the mashed sweet potato, melted nut butter, maple syrup, and cocoa or cacao powder and mix well.
Fold in carob chips.
Pour mixture into greased pan and bake for 20 minutes or until baked through.
Remove from the oven and allow to cool completely before slicing and refrigerating.
These brownies are best when cooled completely. Store in fridge or freezer and ENJOY!

Snowball Cookies

INGREDIENTS
- 1 cup almond butter (cashew, organic peanut butter)
- 2 Tbsp raw honey
- ½ cup carob powder (or cacao or cocoa)
- 2 tsp cinnamon
- 1 tsp nutmeg
- 2 pinches sea salt
- ½ cup dried shredded coconut

Instructions:
Combine all ingredients except coconut in a large bowl and mix thoroughly.
Form into balls and roll in coconut flakes.

Ice Cream

Serves: 4

INGREDIENTS

- **2 large cans of organic full-fat coconut milk**
- **1 frozen banana**
- **4 large dates, pitted**
- **1-2 tsp vanilla extract**
- **pinch of cinnamon**

Instructions:

1. Put the cans of coconut milk in the fridge, turned upside down, to chill overnight. In the morning flip the cans over, open them and pour the liquid at the top of the can into a separate bowl.
2. Scrape the remaining coconut milk fat into a blender as this is the good stuff that we'll use for the recipe.
3. Now combine all of the ingredients into a high-speed blender/food processor and blend until you have a nice thick and creamy consistency. After blending all the ingredients, pour the goodness into a freezer-safe container and give it a good stir every half hour or so to avoid it becoming too solid. You may have to do this 3 or 4 times but it's well worth it.

Berry Coconut Milk Ice Cream

INGREDIENTS

- 1 can of full fat coconut milk
- 1 full cup frozen organic berries of choice
- ¼ tsp stevia
- ½ tsp vanilla extract
- pinch of sea salt

Optional Ingredient:
- 1 scoop of vanilla protein

Instructions:

Blend coconut milk, sweetener, salt, vanilla, and berries until smooth.

Place a sheet of parchment paper on deep baking dish. Pour the coconut milk onto the parchment paper and then freeze for several hours, until hard.

Once frozen, pull the coconut milk off the parchment paper and break into chunks. Add coconut mixture to the blender.

Process until smooth, scooping down the sides as necessary.

4 Ingredient Ice Cream

INGREDIENTS

- 2 bananas, cut into 1-inch slices (frozen)
- ½ cup frozen strawberries, sliced
- 2 Tbsp almond milk
- ½ tsp vanilla

Instructions:

1. Place banana slices on a plate, separating each slice. Place slices in freezer for 2 hours (overnight is best!).
2. Remove strawberries and bananas from freezer and place in food processor, blend until they are the consistency of soft serve ice cream.
3. Add almond milk (more or less for desired texture) and vanilla and blend until smooth and well-mixed.
4. Transfer ice cream to a freezer container and freeze until solid. (Don't have to wait if fruit is frozen, it is like soft serve ice cream.)
5. Scoop with ice cream scoop and serve.

Chocolate Chip Cookies

INGREDIENTS

- 3 cups pecans OR walnuts (soaked overnight, drained, and allowed to air dry)
- 12 Medjool dates, pitted
- 1 tsp orange zest
- 1 tsp cinnamon
- ½ tsp Celtic or Himalayan sea salt (or to taste)
- 1 ½ Tbsp raw coconut oil (best if soft but not liquid)
- 3 Tbsp carob chips or cacao nibs

Instructions:

1. Place dates in food processor with "S" blade and process until smooth.
2. Add walnuts (or pecans), cinnamon, salt, and coconut oil. Process until well blended.
3. Add carob chips and blend just until chips are well distributed.
4. Remove from processor and form tablespoons of mix into balls.
5. Then flatten into round cookies or leave in ball form.

Option: Balls may be rolled in **unsweetened coconut** or **chopped nuts**.

6. Refrigerate till time to serve. ENJOY!

Matcha Pistachio Bliss Balls

INGREDIENTS
- ¾ cup raw cashews
- ¼ cup raw pistachios, shelled
- 6 Medjool dates, pitted
- ¼ cup shredded coconut, unsweetened
- 2 tsp matcha powder
- 1 Tbsp coconut oil
- ¼ cup pistachios, chopped (for rolling)

Instructions:
Place all the ingredients (except the last ¼ cup pistachios) into a food processor. Process for one minute or until finely chopped and blended.

Using an ice cream scoop or tablespoon, scoop out balls of mixture. Roll between your hands to create evenly sized balls.

When all balls have been rolled, roll them again through the chopped pistachios and press firmly into the balls.

Refrigerate for 15 minutes, then enjoy.

Banana Blueberry Muffins

INGREDIENTS
- 3 ripe bananas
- 2 Tbsp melted coconut oil
- 3 Tbsp maple syrup
- ½ tsp baking soda
- ½ tsp baking powder
- 1 ½ cups almond flour
- 1 cup blueberries

Instructions:
Heat oven to 375°. Mash bananas then mix in the rest (except blueberries.) Fold in berries. Use mini muffin tins lined with paper. Fill ¾ full and bake for 15 minutes.

Pumpkin Nut Butter Brownies

Serves: 6-8

- **1 ½ cups pumpkin puree**
- **¾ cup nut butter**
- **¼ cup raw cacao powder**
- **5 dates, pitted**
- **2 cups dark chocolate, melted (at least 60% cacao)**
- **1 cup canned coconut milk**

Instructions:

1. Preheat oven to 350°, and grease a baking pan lightly with coconut oil.
2. Add the pumpkin puree, nut butter, cocoa or cacao powder and dates to a high speed blender or food processor. Pulse just until a thick batter is formed.
3. Pour the mixture into the greased pan and bake for 15-20 minutes, or until a toothpick comes out clean from the center. (Could take up to 20-30 minutes. Put them back in the oven for 5 minutes at a time until done.)
4. Remove from the oven and allow to cool in the pan completely.
5. In a small bowl mix the melted chocolate with coconut milk. Whisk until well combined.
6. Drizzle the chocolate mixture over the brownies, or pour the chocolate mixture on top of the brownies and level it with a spatula.
7. Refrigerate for 3 hours (or overnight).

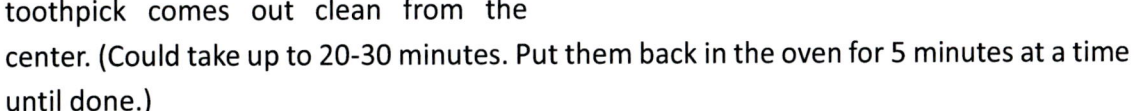

Modified Recipe is from Clean Food Crush

Quinoa Chocolate Banana Bread Recipe

(from Nestandglow.com)

Total time: 1 hr 20 min   Yield: 16 servings

<u>Equipment</u>: Blender, Oven, 8" Baking dish and Greaseproof paper (e.g., parchment paper).

INGREDIENTS

- **2 bananas**
- **1 cup quinoa, soaked overnight**
- **½ cup raisins**
- **½ cup cocoa/cacao powder**
- **½ cup coconut flakes**
- **1 tsp vanilla**
- **3 Tbsp chia seeds, soaked in ½ cup + 1 Tbsp water**
- **pinch of salt**
- **1 cup water**

<u>Topping</u>:

- **2 bananas**
- **2 Tbsp cocoa/cacao powder**
- **2 Tbsp nuts or seeds like hazelnuts or coconut**

<u>Instructions</u>:

1. Soak the quinoa the night before, then drain and rinse.
2. Soak the chia while adding everything for the banana bread into a blender then add the chia last.
3. Blend smooth and pour into a greaseproof paper lined tin.
4. Bake for an hour at 375°F until a toothpick comes out mostly clean.
5. Leave to cool and firm while you make the icing. It will firm up as it cools.
6. Mash two bananas with 2 Tbsp of cacao powder.
7. Spread the icing on the cooled cake and top with chopped nuts or seed.
8. Enjoy within 3 days and keep in the fridge.

Easy and gluten-free banana bread that is sweetened with just fruit. It's oil-free, grain-free, refined sugar-free and nut-free (if you don't decorate with hazelnuts like in the photo).

The basic recipe is for a rich cacao chocolate bread. If you want it sweeter, then double the amount of raisins or add some liquid sweetener. I like my dark chocolate so I just use half a cup of raisins. For non-dark chocolate lovers, you will want to add some more sweetness.

Peanut Butter Protein Bars

INGREDIENTS

- **2 cups rolled oats**
- **¼ cup milled flaxseed**
- **¼ cup ground hemp seeds**
- **15 Medjool dates, pitted & soaked for 1 hr.**
- **1 ½ cups peanut butter (or any nut butter)**
- **½ cup honey**
- **2 Tbsp powdered monk fruit or 1 Tbsp stevia**
- **1 ½ tsp vanilla extract**
- **pinch of salt**
- **Option: ¾ cup vanilla protein powder instead of hemp and flax seeds**

Instructions:
- Spray a glass baking dish with coconut oil cooking spray or line with parchment paper and set aside.
- Place dates in a high-speed food processor or blender. Process on high adding filtered water as needed.
- Add in the rest of the ingredients to your food processor and process on high for 1 to 2 minutes, stopping often to scrape the sides. At this point, the dough should be similar to cookie dough.
- Using your hands, press the dough into the baking dish. Then, use a spatula to make it smooth and even all the way around.
- Pop the baking dish into the freezer for about 30 minutes to set. Remove and then cut into bars with a sharp knife.

Cocoa and Peanut Powder Almond Bars

INGREDIENTS (I usually double the recipe)

- 3 Tbsp coconut oil
- 1 dropper full of liquid stevia
- 2 Tbsp peanut powder
- pinch of sea salt
- 1 Tbsp milled flax seed
- 3 Tbsp raw honey
- 8 Tbsp cocoa OR cacao powder
- ½ tsp concentrated natural vanilla extract
- 2 Tbsp chia seeds
- ½ cup almond slivers

Instructions:

Place all ingredients into a medium sized pan, heat slightly so coconut oil melts and mix until well combined and looking deliciously chocolatey. Stir in the almond slivers. Pour the mixture into a glass container, or plastic if you must (maybe line it with parchment paper). Place in the fridge to set – or even the freezer with a lid on it – it only takes a couple of hours to set; however, the longer you leave it, the firmer it will become. I like it best the day after making.

Cho-Coco Macaroon Bars

INGREDIENTS (I usually double the recipe)

- 3 Tbsp coconut oil
- 1 dropper full of liquid stevia
- 2 Tbsp chia seeds
- pinch of sea salt
- 3 Tbsp raw honey
- 8 Tbsp cocoa OR cacao powder
- ½ tsp concentrated natural vanilla extract
- 1 ½ cups coconut flakes or more

Instructions:

Place all ingredients except for the coconut into a medium sized pan, heat slightly so coconut oil melts. Mix until well combined and looking deliciously chocolatey. Stir in the coconut. Pour the mixture into a glass container, or plastic if you must (maybe line it with parchment paper). Or drop by the tsp so you have the shape of a macaroon cookie. Place in the fridge to set – or even the freezer with a lid on it – it only takes a couple of hours to set. However, the longer you leave it, the firmer it will become. I like it best the day after making.

SNACKS

Extra Green Guacamole

INGREDIENTS

    1 cup of cooked and cooled (or jarred) organic chickpeas
    1 organic lemon, juiced
    organic cilantro – as much or as little as you like
        (I usually use about a small handful)
    2 tsp organic extra virgin olive oil
    ½ avocado
    pink Himalayan salt and pepper to taste
    OPTIONAL: I sometimes spice this up with half of an organic jalapeño,
        with the seeds removed.

Instructions:

You can prepare this dip one of two ways. You can mix the ingredients together by hand in a bowl, or if you want a smoother and creamier consistency, you can chuck everything in a blender for about a minute until everything is combined.

Vegan Spinach Dip

Prep Time: 15 mins   Cook Time: 35 mins   Total Time: 50 mins

Rich, creamy, warm and cheesy Vegan Spinach Dip that makes the perfect appetizer.

by Ceara   Serves: 2 heaping cups

INGREDIENTS

    ½ cup cashews, soaked
    1 medium white onion, diced
    ½ cup frozen spinach (measured after defrosting)
    ¼ cup aquafaba (liquid from the chickpea can)

2 cups cooked or canned chickpeas
2-3 Tbsp nutritional yeast
1 Tbsp tahini
1 tsp apple cider vinegar
2-3 splashes hot sauce
1½ tsp garlic powder
2 tsp onion powder
¼ tsp paprika
1 tsp sea salt (or to taste)
pinch black pepper
chili powder (for garnish, optional)

Instructions:

1. Soak ½ cup cashews overnight or in boiling water for 20 minutes.
2. Preheat oven to 375°F.
3. Over medium-high heat, sauté diced onion in a splash of water (or dollop of oil) for 5 minutes until translucent.
4. Allow frozen spinach to defrost (or microwave on low for 30-second increments) and measure out ½ lightly packed cup of defrosted spinach, pressing out some of the water in the measuring cup.
5. Add soaked cashews, sautéed onion and aquafaba to a high-speed blender (like a Vitamix) and blend until creamy smooth.
6. Add chickpeas, defrosted spinach, nutritional yeast, tahini, apple cider vinegar, hot sauce and spices (garlic and onion powder, paprika, sea salt and pepper) to the blender. Using the tamper, blend for several pulses until the chickpeas are just creamy and still a little bit chunky. If you do not have a high-powered blender, pulse and scrape down the sides so your spices are evenly distributed when blending.
7. Transfer to an oven safe dish and bake for 30 to 35 minutes until the tip of the dip is crispy. Sprinkle with a pinch of chili powder before serving.

Notes:

If you do not have aquafaba on hand, use water or vegetable broth. You may have to adjust the spices and salt a bit to taste if you use water.

Chia Protein Bites

INGREDIENTS

- 2 Tbsp almond butter
- 2 ½ Tbsp raw honey
- 1 Tbsp coconut oil
- 1 scoop of high quality protein powder
- 5 Tbsp raw cacao powder
- pinch of Himalayan pink salt
- 1-2 Tbsp chia seeds

Instructions:

1. Gather ingredients and place into a blender or a bowl.
2. Blend or mix by hand until smooth.
3. Batter will be a little sticky and oily.
4. Scoop batter into bite size balls/cookies and place onto a non-stick surface.
5. Eat right away or store in refrigerator.

Energy Bites

by Kelly H, Ypsilanti MI

INGREDIENTS

- 1 cup dry organic quick oats
- 1/3 cup cacao nibs
- ½ cup almond butter or organic peanut butter
- 1/3 cup raw honey
- ½ cup ground flaxseed
- 1 tsp vanilla (I use Nielsen-Massey pure Madagascar vanilla)

Instructions:

Mix all ingredients together. Batter should be sticky. If it does not hold together well, you might want to add a little more nut butter or honey. Roll into balls. Note: dampening your hands with water will help the batter to not stick to your hands.

Eat energy bites right away or store in refrigerator.

Easy Smooth Hummus

Prep Time: 10 minutes

<u>Why we love this recipe</u>. When we first figured out how to make our own hummus, we were shocked at how easy (and fast) it is. With just a few simple tricks, you really can make creamy smooth hummus at home, and yes, we really do think it's better than store-bought.

<u>What you need to know</u>. Two things here. First, we use canned chickpeas, which is much, much quicker than using dried. Some swear by soaking and cooking their own dried chickpeas, but we're just not that organized and love that canned chickpeas means we can enjoy our hummus in 10 minutes. Second, our recipe calls for tahini, a creamy paste made from sesame seeds. You can usually find tahini in larger grocery stores or specialty markets.

<u>Equipment you'll need</u>. A mesh strainer or colander, food processor, silicone spatula, measuring cups and spoons.

Yield: Makes about 1½ cups or enough for 4 to 6 snack portions

INGREDIENTS

- **one 15-ounce can (425 grams) chickpeas, also called garbanzo beans**
- **¼ cup (59 ml) fresh lemon juice, about 1 large lemon**
- **¼ cup (59 ml) tahini, we use Krinos or homemade tahini (it's easy to make)**
- **half of a large garlic clove, minced**
- **2 Tbsp extra virgin olive oil, plus more for serving**
- **½ to 1 tsp kosher salt, depending on taste**
- **½ tsp ground cumin**
- **2-3 Tbsp water**
- **dash of ground paprika for serving**

<u>Instructions</u>:

Preparing the Hummus

- In the bowl of a food processor, combine tahini and lemon juice. Process for 1 minute. Scrape sides and bottom of bowl, then turn on and process for 30 seconds. This extra time helps "whip" or "cream" the tahini, making smooth and creamy hummus possible.
- Add the olive oil, minced garlic, cumin and the salt to the whipped tahini and lemon

juice mixture. Process for 30 seconds, scrape sides and bottom of bowl, then process another 30 seconds.

Adding the Chickpeas
- Open can of chickpeas, drain liquid then rinse well with water. Add half of the chickpeas to the food processor, then process for 1 minute. Scrape sides and bottom of bowl, add remaining chickpeas and process for 1 to 2 minutes or until thick and quite smooth.

Creating the Perfect Consistency
- Most likely the hummus will be too thick or still have tiny bits of chickpea. To fix this, with the food processor turned on, slowly add 2 - 3 Tablespoons of water until the consistency is perfect.

Kale Chips

INGREDIENTS
- kale, rinsed and dried
- 1 Tbsp olive oil
- 2 Tbsp white balsamic vinegar
- ¼ tsp sea salt

Instructions:
Preheat oven to 350°F.
Remove kale from the stems and tear into bite size pieces. Save the stems for juicing. Lay kale pieces on a lined or greased baking sheet.
In a small bowl, mix oil, vinegar and salt. With a silicone brush, gently brush mixture onto the kale pieces.
Bake in the oven for about 10 minutes or until pieces become crispy. They are so good, I eat the whole tray as soon as they come out! Enjoy!

Baked Kale Chips Recipe (My Favorite)

INGREDIENTS

- 2 bunches kale
- 2 heaping Tbsp almond butter (or any savory nut butter)
- 1 Tbsp extra virgin olive oil
- ½ tsp ground cumin
- ½ tsp chili powder (or substitute curry powder, we make them both ways)
- ½ tsp garlic powder
- 1/8 tsp cayenne pepper
- ½ tsp salt

Instructions:

- Preheat oven to 350°F. Wash the kale and dry thoroughly with paper towels. Pull the leaves off the center ribs in large pieces, and pile on a baking sheet. Discard the ribs.
- In a small bowl mix the nut butter, oil, spices, and salt. Pour over the kale. Use your hands to massage the kale leaves until each one is evenly coated with the spice mixture. You don't want any of the leaves to be drenched in the mixture, so take your time doing this. The more evenly the kale leaves are coated, the better they will bake.
- Lay the kale leaves out flat on 3-4 full sized baking sheets (work in batches if necessary.) Do not overlap. Bake for 10-11 minutes until crisp, but still green. Cool for a few minutes on the baking sheet before moving. If some kale chips are still a little flimsy or damp, remove the crisp chips and place the damp chips back in the oven for a few more minutes. Store in an air-tight container.

Cinnamon Red Hots Tea

By the cup:

- one green tea bag—I like the Kirklands green tea with matcha powder
- 1 small cinnamon stick (3-4 inches)
- 1/16th tsp cayenne pepper

(I typically use cream in this, but not for the 30-Day.)

ESSENTIAL OILS

RECIPES AND MIXTURES

Rosemary Lemon Cashews

INGREDIENTS

- 10 oz raw cashews
- 2 Tbsp extra virgin or light olive oil
- 3 sprigs fresh rosemary (stems removed)
- peel of 1 lemon (zest)
- 4 drops Rosemary oil
- 2-4 drops Lemon oil
- ¾ tsp coarse sea salt

Instructions:

Preheat oven to 375°.

Place nuts on baking sheet and roast for 8-10 minutes.

While nuts are roasting, warm olive oil, fresh rosemary, and lemon zest in skillet over medium heat until sizzling and fragrant. Add cashews.

Remove from heat. Stir in oils and salt. Enjoy!

Fresh Start Bath Soak

INGREDIENTS

(enough for 2 soaks)
- 1 cup Epsom salt
- 1 cup dead sea salt
- ½ cup baking soda
- 10 drops Eucalyptus essential oil
- 10 drops Lavender essential oil
- ½ ounce peppermint leaves

Instructions:

Mix Epsom salt, dead sea salt, and baking soda in large bowl. Stir in peppermint leaves and essential oils thoroughly.

Store in air tight glass container.

** This is a detox soak – so drink plenty of water after a 30-minute soak.**

Bug/Mosquito Spray

INGREDIENTS
- ½ cup distilled water
- 5 drops each of the following essential oils:
    - Purification
    - Lemongrass
    - Palo Santo
    - Citronella

Spider Spray

By Kelly H, Ypsilanti MI

INGREDIENTS to deter spiders and mice

- **1 cup water**
- **15-20 drops of Peppermint oil**

Instructions:

Combine ingredients in a spray bottle. Spray liberally onto a rag and wipe around all windows and doors. Can also be used to wipe down all base boards or anywhere in the house. For even greater effectiveness, also spray liberally around the outdoor perimeter of the house.

Note: Initially, you may notice more spiders, but this is because they are trying to escape the peppermint scent. Once they are eliminated though, you will seldom see any.

Sleep

INGREDIENTS

- **½ cup coconut oil**
  - **15 drops of Cedarwood oil**
  - **15 drops of Lavender oil**
  - **15 drops of Peace & Calming oil**

Pain Relief

INGREDIENTS

- **1 cup coconut oil**
- **10 drops each of the following essential oils:**
  - **Valor**
  - **PanAway**
  - **Peppermint**
  - **Copaiba**
  - **Lemongrass**

IMMUNITY SUPPORT

12 Natural Remedies for Conquering the Common Cold?

1) Vitamin D
2) Apple cider vinegar
3) Vitamin C
4) Honey
5) Ginger
6) Zinc
7) Echinacea
8) Neti Pot
9) Oregano oil
10) Coconut oil
11) Cinnamon
12) Elderberry (see suggestions next page)

What if You Have a Cold?

- STAY HYDRATED. Water, juice, clear broth, or warm lemon water with honey helps loosen congestion and prevents dehydration. Stay away from alcohol, coffee, and caffeinated sodas, which can make dehydration worse.
- REST. Your body needs to heal.
- A SALTWATER GARGLE can soothe a sore throat—Dissolve ¼ to ½ tsp salt dissolved in an 8-ounce glass of warm water—can temporarily relieve a sore or scratchy throat. You can also try ice chips, sore throat sprays, lozenges, or hard candy.
- Over-the-counter SALINE NASAL DROPS and sprays can help relieve stuffiness and congestion.
- SIP WARM LIQUIDS. A cold remedy used in many cultures, taking in warm liquids, such as soup, tea, or warm fresh apple juice, might be soothing and ease congestion by increasing mucus flow.
- ADD MOISTURE TO THE AIR. A cool-mist vaporizer or humidifier can add moisture to your home, which might help loosen congestion. Change the water daily and clean the unit according to the manufacturer's instructions.

Natural Cold or Flu Medicine

Frankincense essential oil can help provide relief from coughing. It can help eliminate phlegm in the lungs. It also acts as an anti-inflammatory in the nasal passages, making breathing easier, even for those with allergies or asthma. Add a few drops to a cloth and inhale for the respiratory benefits or use an oil diffuser.

Energy C with Electrolytes from www.swansonvitamins.com

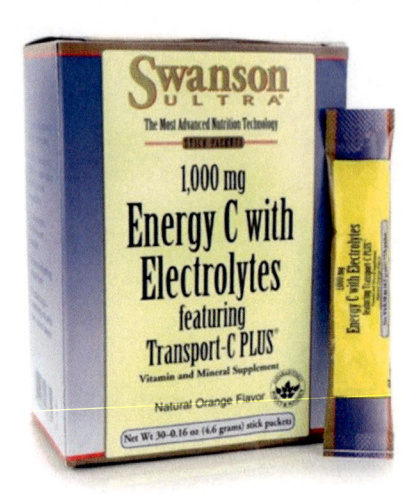

Sambucus Elderberry Syrup

Sambucol – Black Elderberry

Cold Prevention
- Keep your nose area warm
- Wash your hands regularly—especially before eating or touching your eyes, nose or mouth
- Stick to a diet filled with plants and vegetables

Immunity Green Smoothie
By Katrine van Wyk, author of "Best Green Drinks Ever" (see recipe on page 22)

Apple Cider Vinegar (ACV)
Use organic, raw, unpasteurized ACV with "the mother" on the label for all the benefits.
ACV can help with weight loss and to avoid getting sick.
ACV with honey can treat ailments, including coughs and colds.

How ACV Works
- Drinking a glass of water with a tablespoon of apple cider vinegar before a meal helps to curb your appetite. It also helps stimulate hydrochloric acid, which we need to break down our foods for further absorption and digestion.
- It can help control your blood sugar.
- It contains several antioxidants, which are great for you because they boost your body's immune system and help you fight off illness.
- Combined with a balanced diet, it helps regulate your pH levels. We want a mildly alkaline environment to stave off disease, including cancer, autoimmunity and the common cold.
- It is high in is acetic acid, which helps your body absorb minerals.

ACV Immunity Booster Tea

by Andrea Johnson

INGREDIENTS

- **1 tsp apple cider vinegar**
- **1 cup green tea**
- **a squeeze of lemon juice**
- **a drop or 2 of raw honey**
- **1 small slice of ginger**
- **a dash of Ceylon cinnamon**

Instructions:

1. Steep the tea in water for 2-3 minutes.
2. Remove tea and stir in the remaining ingredients. *The longer the ginger steeps the stronger it will be.
3. Remove ginger slice before drinking.

Kick it Up Salad Dressing

by Andrea Johnson

INGREDIENTS

- **½ tsp liquid Stevia**
- **¼ cup apple cider vinegar**
- **¼ cup extra virgin olive oil**
- **1 teaspoon red pepper**
- **juice from 1 lemon**
- **salt and pepper to taste (you can also use black seeds for the pepper)**

Instructions:

1. Whisk together Stevia, apple cider vinegar, lemon juice and red pepper.
2. Slowly pour in olive oil while whisking to emulsify.
3. Season with salt and pepper to taste.
4. Pour into jar with lid and refrigerate. Makes about ½ cup.

Lose It Salad Dressing

by Andrea Johnson

INGREDIENTS

- ⅓ cup extra virgin olive oil
- 2 Tbsp apple cider vinegar
- 3-4 drops liquid Stevia
- ½ Tbsp Bragg's liquid aminos
- 1 tsp finely ground flax seeds
- a dash of salt
- ¼ tsp black pepper (you can also use black seeds)
- ¼ tsp red pepper
- ½ small clove of garlic, finely grated on a microplane

Instructions:

1. Whisk together all ingredients until mixed.
2. Pour into jar with lid and refrigerate.
3. Makes about ⅓ cup.

Blueberries

THE CANCER-FIGHTING IMMUNITY BOOSTER

- Contain cancer-fighting antioxidants for immunity
- Increase metabolism and regulate blood sugar levels
- Promote cell regeneration for healthy, youthful skin
- Protect heart health and prevent osteoporosis
- Support digestive health, weight loss, and circulation

12 Suggestions for General Immunity Support

1. Get adequate rest
2. Drink half your body weight in ounces of filtered water
3. Add 2 drops of organic lemon oil to a large glass of warm filtered water, and drink every morning
4. Exercise at least a little bit daily; walk, stretch—keep your body active
5. Eat a healthy diet; incorporate many of the recipes from this book into your diet and eliminate sugar as much as possible
6. Pursue and maintain a healthy body weight
7. Use a good probiotic daily and consider using a detox kit quarterly
8. Take steps to reduce toxins in and around your home
9. Take a digestive enzyme whenever you eat cooked food
10. Take a vitamin D-3 supplement and take an iodine supplement such as kelp
11. Reduce stress
12. Seek God for inner peace and unity with Him

The Author

LIFESTYLE COACH: LILLIAN EASTERLY-SMITH

Motivational Speaker,
    Co-Author of *Fit 'n' Faith*,
        Lifestyle/ Health Coach,
            Fitness Instructor,
                Counselor,

LILLIAN EASTERLY-SMITH is passionate about helping people make lifestyle changes that last—devoting her time to help others enjoy fullness of life—body, soul & spirit through the experience and knowledge she and her husband, Mike Smith, have gleaned over 12+ years of study and practice. If you are confused, tired of trying fad diets, feel overwhelmed with contradictory information and lack motivation, what they have to offer is for you! Mike & Lillian offer:

- personal coaching via face-to-face meetings that includes a nutrition assessment
- personal coaching by phone or video chat
- a private Facebook / video group course
- a Baby-Step Program in their recent book release, *Fit 'n' Faith*
- as well as a 30-Day Jumpstart Challenge.

Studies have proven that setting goals, developing a plan and having accountability bring results. Coaching can assist you in making lifestyle changes!

The Contributors

PHARMACIST: DEANNA CATALANO

DEANNA CATALANO, graduate of Massachusetts College of Pharmacy, has been in the pharmacy profession for 22 + years. During those years of practice, Deanna has seen a need for more options for people wanting to live a healthy lifestyle. In October of 2018, she met Lillian Easterly-Smith and her husband, Mike Smith. Since then, Deanna has worked with Lillian and Mike to bring healthier living options and education to the community and surrounding areas. They offer health seminars for those that are interested or just curious about the path to healthier living. This led to the idea and reality of a recipe book that provides people with healthy, easy ideas to incorporate into their busy lives.

AUTHOR: KELLY HAWKINS

KELLY HAWKINS, along with her husband, is a former owner of two Anytime Fitness gyms. Kelly has valued fitness her whole life but in more recent years has more carefully considered the foods we put in our bodies. She has been on a learning journey regarding true health and wellness alongside Lillian for the past 12 years. Having so many family members who have faced cancer and heart disease, she is constantly pursuing ways to live more healthfully and lead others in more healthful living in order to fulfill all we were created to be and do in this life.
Kelly leads fitness classes through LifeCare Christian Center. She also considers herself an innovative cook since she loves to develop new and creative recipes, some of which have found their way into this book.

Thank you to those of you who submitted recipes for this book. Your delicious contributions are a labor of love that will benefit many!

Made in the USA
Lexington, KY
27 July 2019